O9-AHW-104

THE HANDBOOK OF THE
FORMER SOVIET UNION

The
MILLBROOK
Reference
Library

THE HANDBOOK OF THE
FORMER
SOVIET
UNION

MICHAEL G. KORT

THE MILLBROOK PRESS
Brookfield, Connecticut

J947
KOR

Photographs courtesy of Sovfoto/TASS: pp. 25, 72, 86, 106, 205; © 1996 Bill Gasperini, Impact Visuals: p. 41; © Robert S. Semeniuk: pp. 45, 49; Sovfoto: pp. 55, 167; © Robert Wallis/SABA: p. 60; Sovfoto/Novosti: pp. 78, 126, 199; © Markku Ulander/Lehtikuva Oy/SABA: p. 83; Ergûn Çagatay: pp. 112 (I. Voljinski), 118 (I. Vvedensky); © Shepard Sherbell/ SABA: p. 132; AP/Wide World Photos: pp. 152 (both), 160, 164, 165, 170, 173, 176, 178, 179, 184 (both), 192, 208, 227, 236; ITAR-TASS/Sovfoto: pp. 153, 154, 161, 171, 182 (both), 183, 190, 191, 198, 204, 215, 219 (top), 220, 232 (both), 237; RIA-Novosti/Sovfoto: pp. 155, 175; UPI/Corbis-Bettmann: pp. 157, 159; Reuters/Corbis-Bettmann: pp. 158, 180, 196; Agence France Presse/Corbis-Bettmann: pp. 185, 186; © M. Seppanen-Helin/Lehtikova Oy/SABA: p. 216; CTK/Eastfoto: p. 219 (bottom).

Library of Congress Cataloging-in-Publication Data
Kort, Michael
The handbook of the former Soviet Union/by Michael Kort.
p.   cm.
Includes bibliographical references and index.
Summary: Looks at the past, present, and future of all the newly
independent nations of the former Soviet Union, with a chronology
of events leading up to the fall of the Soviet Union.
ISBN 0–7613–0016–3 (lib. bdg.)
1. Former Soviet republics—Juvenile literature. [1. Former Soviet republics.]
DK293.K667 1997   947—dc20   96–36472 CIP AC

The Millbrook Reference Library

Published by The Millbrook Press, Inc.
2 Old New Milford Road, Brookfield, Connecticut 06804

Copyright © 1997 by Michael G. Kort
Printed in the United States of America
All rights reserved
1   3   5   6   4   2

FOR THE KORT BROTHERS

*In memory of Victor, my father,
and my uncles Edward and Otto,
and in honor of my uncle Alfred.*

CONTENTS

PREFACE

In the waning days of 1991, the Union of Soviet Socialist Republics collapsed. The rapid unraveling of the world's largest country and one of two nuclear superpowers occurred with a suddenness that stunned the world. Taking the Soviet Union's place in the vast territory of northern Eurasia were fifteen independent countries. The giant Russian Federation, the core of the former Soviet empire, still spanned the breadth of northern Eurasia. Lithuania, Latvia, and Estonia hugged the coast of the Baltic Sea. Ukraine, Belarus, and Moldova lay west of Russia on the broad plains of Eastern Europe. Georgia, Armenia, and Azerbaijan were wedged into the Transcaucasus region between the Black and Caspian seas where Europe and Asia meet. And Kazakhstan, Uzbekistan, Turkmenistan, Kyrgyzstan, and Tajikistan shared unequal parts of Central Asia's dusty steppe, baking deserts, and rugged mountains.

The Soviet Union's collapse brought self-determination to tens of millions of people. It created the potential for national development that had been smothered for centuries by both the Soviet Union and the Russian Empire that had preceded it. At the same time, the Soviet Union's demise created an enormous power vacuum and dangerous instability.

It left behind a collection of struggling countries with enormous political, social, economic, and environmental problems. It also left a vast region of the world ravaged by ethnic discord. In short, the emergence of fifteen new countries where one had existed before, while creating new opportunity, presented many new problems without solving old ones.

Eleven of the new countries belonged to the vaguely defined and loosely structured Commonwealth of Independent States (CIS), which was hastily organized in December 1991 to replace the dying Soviet Union. (Lithuania, Latvia, Estonia, and Georgia did not join.) While the purpose of the CIS was to foster cooperation among the Soviet successor states, in reality there was no shared vision of what it should do. Over the next several years it served mainly as a vehicle for the giant Russian Federation to assert its influence on the smaller CIS members.

This handbook will introduce you to each of the countries that were formerly part of the Soviet Union, all of which now belong to the United Nations. It will provide an overview of their people, geography, history, culture, and current problems. It also contains a chronology of the events leading up to the collapse of the Soviet Union, and the events that followed. The third section is an encyclopedia of key people, topics, and significant events. With this book, you will be able to better understand the prospects and problems that the countries of northern Eurasia face.

There is more than one way to spell many of the names in this book. We have used what we feel are the most common spellings. In the case of Belarus, note that in the Soviet Era, pre-1991, the region was known as Belorussia. Today the people of this country are known as Belarusians.

CHAPTER ONE

THE EURASIAN COLOSSUS

From the mid-1600s until the end of 1991, a gigantic country, by far the largest in the world, sprawled across northern Eurasia. At its peak it covered about 8.5 million square miles (22 million square kilometers), almost one sixth of the Earth's entire land area. It included half of Europe and half of Asia, spanning 6,000 miles (9,656 kilometers) from west to east. At its widest point it stretched more than 2,000 miles (3,200 kilometers) from the ice-choked waters of the Arctic Ocean in the north to parched desert plains of Central Asia in the south. Canada and China, the world's second- and third-largest nations, would have fit easily side by side inside its borders, with more than enough room left over to wedge in a territory the size of Alaska.

During those three centuries, this Eurasian colossus had three different names: Muscovy, Russia, and the Union of Soviet Socialist Republics (or Soviet Union). Over the centuries its borders gradually expanded, although they also shrank at times when its power declined. War and revolution changed its form of government and its social and economic systems. After 1917 monarchs who claimed to draw their authority from God were replaced by commissars whose claim to power came from the theories of a philosopher named Karl Marx. A budding capitalist free-market system was uprooted and replaced by the world's first socialist economy, a system under which the government owns a country's factories, businesses, and farms, and plans and controls most economic activities. A country that for most of its history was largely agricultural eventually became one of the world's leading industrial powers.

Yet despite these important changes, some fundamental characteristics of the colossal Muscovite/Russian/Soviet state remained the same. Its government was always dictatorial, whether ruled by absolute monarchs called tsars or by leaders of the Communist Party, an organization that claimed to represent ordinary workers and peasants. Although many nationalities and ethnic groups lived within the country's vast borders, it was dominated by one group, the Russians (or, as they are sometimes called, the Great Russians). Because of the country's huge size, it was feared by its many neighbors in both Europe and Asia. Despite its size, it feared them. When it suffered defeat in war, no matter how severe, it always managed somehow to recover and hold together. And yet, despite seemingly endless sacrifices by its people and immense effort by its government, it was always poor.

THE PHYSICAL SETTING: THE EURASIAN PLAIN

The natural setting of the former Soviet Union was the vast Eurasian Plain. Its European portion, called the North European Plain, begins at the Atlantic shore and extends across the continent to a band of rolling hills called the Ural Mountains, where Europe ends and Asia begins. From Asia's western edge, the lowlands, now called the West Siberian Plain, continue for about 1,200 miles (1,930 kilometers) before rising to become the Central Siberian Plateau. The land continues to rise until it becomes the Verkhoyansk, Chersky, and Kolyma mountain ranges, before sloping downward to become the rocky shore of the Pacific Ocean.

The territory once occupied by the former Soviet Union is bounded in the north by the Arctic Ocean. Its southern limits are marked, approximately rather than precisely, by a combination of mountains and seas. In Europe, the Carpathian Mountains, the Black Sea, and the Caucasus Mountains frame the Eurasian plane. In Asia, the Caspian Sea, the world's largest inland body of water, gives way to a series of uplands and mountain ranges that extend northeast for more than 3,000 miles (4,828 kilometers).

The Eurasian Plain and its surrounding highlands are laced by an elaborate network of rivers. The most important rivers on the European part of the former Soviet Union are the Dnieper, the Don, and the Volga, all of which flow generally from north to south. In Asia, the mighty Ob, Yenisey, and Lena flow in the opposite direction, emptying their waters into the Arctic Ocean. Among the major lakes in the former Soviet Union are Ladoga and Onega in the northwest, the salty Aral Sea in Central Asia, and Lake Baikal in the mountains of Central Siberia.

This huge region has four major vegetation zones. In the far north is the tundra, a region of semifrozen soil covered by mosses, lichens, and stunted shrubs able to survive in arctic climates. As one moves southward the tundra gives way to the largest forest in the world, which covers an area greater than that of the United States. South of the forest is the steppe, a broad prairie similar to the American Great Plains, but not as well watered. The "black earth" of the steppe is among the world's most fertile soils. South of the steppe in the Central Asian part of the plain is a large desert region.

THE ORIGINS OF THE RUSSIAN EURASIAN STATE

The Russians, who built the state that eventually grew to span all of northern Eurasia, trace their origins to a group of people known in history as the East Slavs. Today's Ukrainians and Belarusians also trace their origins to the East Slavs. Approximately 1,500 years ago, the East Slavs first settled the steppe and forest of what today is Ukraine, Belarus, and the western part of Russia. In the ninth century the East Slavs were organized in a state centered at Kiev, a city on the lower Dnieper River. Kievian Rus, as it was called, was really a loose union of principalities whose princes often fought against one another as well as against foreign foes. In the tenth century Prince Vladimir of Kiev was converted to Eastern Orthodox Christianity, which became the religion of Kievian Rus and most of the East Slavs.

Kievian Rus produced a rich culture that compared favorably to that of the other states of Europe. Kiev itself was a city of many beautiful churches, as was the vibrant northern trading city of Novgorod. Other important cities included Rostov and Ryazan. In these cities, the princes shared power with the nobility and with town assemblies called *veches*. A rich religious literature developed that included hymns, sermons, and tales of saints. At the same time, a largely secular literature was being composed. *The Primary Chronicle*, a mixture of myth and historical record, was written down in the twelfth century. It is the best source for the history of Kievian Rus between 800 and 1100. The most famous example of secular literature from the Kievian era is *The Tale of the Host of Igor*, a beautiful and tragic epic poem about a disastrous Kievian campaign against nomads of the steppe.

After several centuries of relative power and prosperity, Kievian Rus weakened. In the thirteenth century it was conquered and destroyed by the Mongols (or Tatars, as the Russians called them), fierce and brutal nomadic invaders from inner Asia. The Mongol conquest devastated the land and was followed by more than two centuries of oppressive foreign rule over the region.

During the era of Mongol rule, three distinct national groups evolved in what had once been Kievian Rus: the Russians, Ukrainians, and Belarusians. The Russians, the largest of those groups, lived most directly under Mongol control. The Belarusians and Ukrainians evolved under the influence of two expanding powers to the west: Poland and Lithuania.

The Mongol conquest and its aftermath retarded the region's economic development. Meanwhile, local people fled the open steppe near Kiev for the greater security of the forest regions in the north. This helped to strengthen the northern Russian principalities, including a tiny state called Muscovy, centered around the city of Moscow. Muscovy also benefited by its location near the sources of several major rivers, which gave it control over important trade routes. Because its princes succeeded in winning the favor of the Mongol ruler, the dreaded khan, Muscovy's rulers became more powerful than rival Russian princes. Muscovy then was able to expand its territory at the expense of its neighbors. Once a tiny backwater principality, Muscovy gradually but relentlessly began to grow larger and stronger. It also became the seat of the Russian Orthodox Church, and therefore an important place to all Russians, wherever they lived.

The Mongol khan's example of exercising absolute power over his subjects provided a model for the Russian princes under his control, including the prince of Muscovy. During the fourteenth and fifteenth centuries, Moscow's princes dramatically increased their power over their subjects. The most successful of those early princes, Ivan III, appropriately known as Ivan the Great, significantly weakened the country's nobility. Ivan also succeeded in fulfilling a dream more than two centuries old when in 1480 he declared Muscovy's independence from Mongol rule.

By the time Ivan died in 1505, Muscovy had absorbed all the territories of its Russian rivals and had grown into the largest state in Europe. Expansion continued under Ivan's successors, especially his grandson Ivan IV, better known as Ivan the Terrible, a name he well deserved. Ivan the Terrible crushed the last opposition to his absolute rule and, in 1547, had himself crowned "tsar (the Russian word for Caesar) of all the Russians." His most effective weapon against his opponents was a new innovation, a political police force called the *oprichnina*. Ivan also led Russia on a campaign of conquest toward the east. His forces overran territories in the eastern part of Europe, crossed the Urals into Asia, and began the momentous conquest of Siberia. These conquests, which extended to the Pacific coast by the mid-seventeenth century, for the first time brought significant numbers of non-Russians under Russian control. They also made Russia the largest country in the world.

Russia's enormous expansion did not benefit ordinary Russians, most of whom were peasants. At first, as new lands were conquered in the east, Russian peasants were able to move to get away from oppressive landlords or taxes. However, this caused problems for the country's landlords, who found themselves without enough peasant laborers to work their estates. In order to guarantee that landlords would have laborers to farm their estates, the Russian monarchs gradually began to limit the peasants' right to move. Over a period of about 150 years in the sixteenth and seventeenth centuries, the peasants lost their freedom and the Russian system of serfdom was created.

Most Russians had to serve their noble landlords and the tsar. To the nobles they owed unpaid labor; to the tsar they owed high taxes and their sons, who were conscripted to serve in his army. The nobles, in turn, had no rights against the power of the tsar. Russia meanwhile was becoming a multinational empire as continued expansion brought the tsar many unwilling non-Russian subjects. By the early seventeenth century, the autocratic Russian Eurasian state that would dominate northern Eurasia for 350 years was in place.

THE RUSSIAN EMPIRE

After a period of turmoil and weakness, a new dynasty called the Romanovs took over the Russian throne in 1613. The Romanov dynasty would rule Russia until the monarchy collapsed in 1917. The outstanding early Romanov tsar was Peter I, known as Peter the Great, who ruled from 1689 to 1725. Peter was a giant both historically and physically: he stood almost 7 feet (214 centimeters) tall. He had himself crowned emperor in 1721, thereby officially inaugurating the era of the Russian Empire. He continued Russia's expansion westward into Europe and eastward into Asia. One of his achievements was the conquest of part of the Baltic Coast, where he built St. Petersburg, which would remain Russia's capital until 1918. On the other side of Eurasia, Peter negotiated a border and trade agreement with the Chinese Empire. Peter also tightened the rules governing serfdom, and used his newly organized political police force to crush any potential opposition to his policies. He also was the first Russian ruler to actively promote economic and industrial development.

Peter's successors continued Russia's expansion while they preserved the power of the throne. Catherine the Great (1762–1796) pushed Russia's borders westward into Poland and southward to the Black Sea. By the end of her reign, all of what today is Belarus and Ukraine was in Russian hands. Shortly after the turn of the century, Russia annexed what today is Moldova, which had been under Turkish control. Russian power reached and crossed the Caucasus Mountains during the first half of the nineteenth century, although bitter resistance to Russian rule continued for decades. Large tracts of land in the Far East were taken from China between 1858 and 1860, and Central Asia fell to Russian expansion in the 1860s and 1870s. Russia even expanded into the Americas, occupying Alaska during the late eighteenth and early nineteenth centuries, and reaching as far south as the San Francisco area of California. However, the California possessions were too far away to be held for long, and Alaska was sold to the United States in 1867.

By the end of the nineteenth century, about one half of the population of the Russian Empire was made up of non-

Russians. Some groups were large nations like Poland, numbering millions of people. Others were small tribes, among them various Siberian peoples. Altogether, the empire contained more than a hundred distinct national or ethnic groups. As a result, some critics referred to Russia as "the prison house of nations."

Meanwhile, all this expansion could not solve or cover up a serious problem inside the Russian Empire. Ever since the Mongol conquest, Russia had lagged behind Western Europe in economic and technological development. This backwardness was dangerous because technological and economic strength is quickly translated into military power. Both Ivan the Terrible and Peter the Great had suffered military defeats against modern Western European armies. After his defeat by Sweden in 1700, Peter launched a concerted effort to modernize Russia, but with limited success.

After 1850, Russia's tsars launched several major reform programs to overcome their empire's backwardness. The first came after Russia's defeat in the Crimean War of 1853–1856, a loss attributed in part to its lack of railroads and adequate supplies. Five years after the war ended, Tsar Alexander II abolished serfdom. Alexander's other reforms included overhauling local government, education, the judicial system, and the military. Between 1892 and 1903, the governments of Alexander III and Nicholas II actively promoted industrialization. Russia's subsequent defeat in the Russo-Japanese War of 1904–1905 led to a major upheaval in Russia known as the Revolution of 1905, which threatened to bring down the Romanov dynasty. In 1905, with his throne teetering on the brink of collapse, Tsar Nicholas II reluctantly issued the October Manifesto, under which Russia would elect a parliament with limited powers the following year. This reform, along with brutal repression after the Russian armies returned from fighting the Japanese in the Far East, enabled Nicholas II and the monarchy to survive. Major agricultural reforms followed during the next few years.

Some Russians accepted neither the old order nor the reforms of Alexander II and Nicholas II. By the 1860s, tiny groups of revolutionaries were beginning to organize, determined to overthrow the tsar. The revolutionaries were inspired by various socialist ideas, although they often disagreed with one another as strongly as they opposed the tsar. One extremely important characteristic shared by many of these revolutionaries is that while opposing autocratic tsarism, they also rejected democracy. They said they wanted all Russians to be equal, but believed that only a socialist dictatorship they controlled could accomplish this goal. Despite their fervor, the revolutionary socialists could do little to overthrow the tsar. When Russia exploded in the Revolution of 1905, the revolutionaries took a leading role in the struggle, but were crushed when the Russian armies returned from the Far East at the end of the Russo-Japanese War.

Nicholas II and the Russian monarchy did not long survive their victory. In 1914, World War I broke out and Nicholas II again led his country into war. Less than three years later, reeling from bitter military defeats at the front and terrible suffering at home, the Russian people overthrew Nicholas II and the monarchy. An attempt to establish a democratic government collapsed after eight months. Taking advantage of the chaos into which Russia had fallen, a small socialist party called the Bolsheviks seized power and established a one-party dictatorship. In 1922 they chose a new name for the country: the Union of Soviet Socialist Republics.

THE SOVIET ERA

The Bolsheviks, led to power in 1917 by Vladimir Lenin, were socialists who believed in the ideas of a nineteenth-century German thinker named Karl Marx. They hated capitalism, which they said was a system in which a few rich, who owned all the wealth of a society, oppressed and exploited everyone else. They wanted to establish a socialist society in which all wealth would be shared equally. Eventually they believed socialism could be made to work so well that the perfect society would exist, a state of affairs Marx called communism.

As Marxists, the Bolsheviks believed that they were the leaders of Russia's working class. They also accepted the Marxist view that a violent revolution was necessary to overthrow capitalism and establish socialism. Following Lenin's theories, the Bolsheviks, unlike some other Marxists, also were convinced that a one-party dictatorship was necessary to build socialism. That is why the Bolsheviks overthrew the democratic government set up early in 1917 and replaced it with a dictatorship. Within a month after seizing power the Bolsheviks set up a secret police to silence their political opponents. They retained power in the murderous and destructive civil war that followed between 1918 and 1921.

Although the Bolsheviks, who renamed themselves the Communist Party in 1918, wanted to build the world's first socialist society, they moved slowly during their first decade in power. Large industries were taken over by the state, and land belonging to large landholders was seized and distributed among the peasants. However, the government did not interfere in the lives of the peasants, the large majority of the population. They continued to farm their land as they did in the past. In other words, most people continued to live and work much as they had before the revolution. That was the situation when Lenin died in 1924.

Joseph Stalin won the struggle for power in the years immediately after Lenin's death. Under Stalin's dictatorial leadership, the Soviet regime began a program of rapid industrialization designed to make the Soviet Union equal to the advanced countries of the West. The program changed the way most Soviet citizens lived. It was carried out with a brutality that would have impressed Ivan the Terrible and Peter the Great. The government seized all the peasants' land and forced them onto government-controlled collective farms, where dozens or hundreds of families worked the land together. Because the peasants resisted the seizure of their land, and because Stalin's government would stop at nothing to break their will, an estimated ten million peasants died as a result of collectivization. The regime also began a series of five-year plans, under which all resources went to build industries like steel, coal, machine tools, and armaments. Little was left over for the people, and the Soviet Union experienced the greatest peacetime standard-of-living decline of any country in history.

On top of that, in the mid-1930s, Stalin launched a reign of terror called the "Great Purge" designed to establish his absolute power. Millions of people were arrested for no reason and either were shot or sent to labor camps, where a great many of them died. The huge network of labor camps was called the *gulag*. As a result of these developments, a new type of state emerged: the totalitarian state. The totalitarian state uses modern technology and organization to exercise firm and pervasive control over the lives of the people, far greater control than was possible by even the most oppressive regimes of earlier centuries. The press, all cultural institutions, churches, and schools, and even sports and recreational institutions all fall under state control.

The Soviet Union was not the only totalitarian state of its time; Nazi Germany was another. And there have been others since, such as the People's Republic of China. But few have exceeded either the control or the brutality of Stalin's totalitarian regime. The dictatorial state that had existed under the tsars, even at its worst, was mild by comparison. During the late nineteenth and early twentieth centuries, Russia had been changing and slowly becoming more like the nations of Western Europe. The policies of the Communists under Lenin and especially under Stalin reversed this trend and brought Russia's grim tradition of oppressive government to its worst extreme ever.

Stalin's brutal campaigns were interrupted by World War II. Between 1941 and 1945 the Soviet Union fought a life-and-death struggle with Nazi Germany. Although the Soviet Union joined the United States, Great Britain, and their allies on the winning side, the war left much of the western part of the country in ruins and more than 20 million of its people dead.

After Stalin's death in 1953, the Soviet regime became significantly less harsh under his successors. Nikita Khrushchev, who led the country from 1953 to 1964, introduced reforms to raise the standard of living and end the terroristic methods used to control the people in Stalin's day. But the Soviet totalitarian state, while milder than in Stalin's day, still controlled the country and the people's lives. Khrushchev's reform program, limited as it was, was brought to a sudden end when the rest of the Communist Party leadership turned against him and removed him from office. The new Soviet leader, Leonid Brezhnev (1964–1982), then reversed some of Khrushchev's reforms.

Regardless of which Communist Party boss led the country, however, the Soviet totalitarian state proved to be inefficient and unable to provide a decent life for the Soviet people, especially in comparison to life in the West. By the 1980s, the Soviet economy was in crisis, and corruption and despair continued to grow in Soviet society.

Meanwhile, one feature of the way the Soviet Union was organized eventually had an unexpected effect on how the dust would settle when the Soviet Union eventually collapsed. Although the Communist Party continued to control the non-Russian nationalities tightly from Moscow, its leaders did not want to admit that this practice made them little different from the tsars they hated. The Soviet leaders also wanted to find a more efficient way to rule their huge country. The Soviet Union therefore was organized into fifteen "union" republics, one for each of the country's major national groups.

Russia, comprising three quarters of the Soviet Union, was by far the largest republic. Because it contained a large number of additional subdivisions for minority ethnic groups, the Russian republic was officially called the Russian Soviet Federated Socialist Republic (RSFSR). Among the other union republics, each of which was called a Soviet Socialist Republic (SSR), were the Belorussian SSR (the Soviet-era name for Belarus), the Ukrainain SSR, and Kazakhstan SSR.

The Soviet leadership had no intention of allowing the non-Russian peoples self-determination. Its main goal was to Russify as many of the non-Russian nationalities as possible, especially Slavic groups closely related to the Russians, like the Belarusians and Ukrainians. Among the Russification policies the Soviet regime used was a requirement that all Soviet students learn the Russian language in school. More than 90 percent of all Soviet newspapers were printed in Russian, as were about 85 percent of magazines and periodicals and books.

However, creating the union republics tended to work against Russification: Their existence in many cases reinforced the various national identities of the non-Russians. This remained a serious problem for the Soviet leadership as long as the Soviet Union existed. When the Soviet Union collapsed, the republics became the basis for the fifteen new countries that emerged from the wreckage.

GORBACHEV, REFORM, AND THE COLLAPSE OF THE SOVIET UNION

In 1985 a new leader came to power. Mikhail Gorbachev was determined to reform the Soviet system. His main goal was to overhaul the economy, but he soon found that he could not fix the economy without making other reforms as well. Gorbachev realized that he would have to begin telling the Soviet people the truth about conditions in their country. He was forced to make democratic reforms in order to rally to his cause millions of ordinary Soviet citizens outside the Communist Party.

Gorbachev hoped to allow just a little openness and freedom, and to use the support they brought him to rebuild the Soviet economy. But a little openness and freedom quickly led to demands for more, and within a few years Gorbachev, like the sorcerer's apprentice in the Walt Disney film, lost control of what he had started. Meanwhile, the Soviet economy crumbled faster than Gorbachev could rebuild it. And, most dangerously, some non-Russian nationalities began to demand first limited self-government and then complete freedom.

The pace and scope of change he could no longer control led Gorbachev to permit elections in the spring of 1989, in which non-Communists could compete, on a limited basis, for seats in a new Soviet parliament called the Congress of People's Deputies. The openness of the campaign and its results shocked almost everybody. Non-Communists won 20 percent of the seats, running especially well in non-Russian regions. A year later, Communist Party candidates were defeated across the country in local elections. By the summer of 1991, the Soviet Union was sinking into chaos.

In August, old-line Communists opposed to Gorbachev's reforms briefly overthrew him. While Gorbachev was on vacation at a Black Sea resort, they put him under house arrest and seized control in Moscow. The world waited breathlessly as the Soviet Union teetered on the brink of civil war. The coup against Gorbachev failed, however, in large part because reformers rallied around Boris Yeltsin, an ex-Communist leader who had criticized Gorbachev for moving too slowly with his reforms. Shortly before the coup, Yeltsin had been elected president of the Russian republic, making him the first freely elected leader in Russia's history. On the first day of the coup, Yeltsin dramatically climbed on top of a tank outside his headquarters and rallied reformist forces. Hundreds of thousands of people massed in the streets of Moscow and Leningrad. Faced with unexpected opposition and unsure whether the army would shoot, the anti-Gorbachev plotters hesitated. Foreign leaders, including United States President George Bush, expressed strong support for Gorbachev and Yeltsin. Within three days the coup against Gorbachev collapsed.

It was only a matter of months, though, before the Soviet Union fell apart. Again Yeltsin took the leading role. He brought together leaders from other republics to form the very vaguely defined Commonwealth of Independent States (CIS). Yeltsin first met with the presidents of Ukraine and Belarus on December 8, 1991, in the Belarus capital of Minsk, where

In a photo seen around the world, Yeltsin stands atop a tank outside the parliament building on that fateful day in August 1991.

the three leaders announced the establishment of the new CIS. On December 21, that decision was confirmed and expanded when eleven republics—the original three plus Moldova, Armenia, Azerbaijan, Kazakhstan, Uzbekistan, Turkmenistan, Kyrgyzstan, and Tajikistan—officially became cofounders of the CIS at a meeting in Alma-Ata, the capital of Kazakhstan.

Mikhail Gorbachev, as the Soviet president, opposed the dissolution of the Soviet Union but could do nothing to prevent it. On December 25, Gorbachev resigned his post, and on December 31 the Soviet Union was officially abolished. In its place were fifteen new independent nations, eleven of which belonged to the hastily organized Commonwealth of Independent States. How these new nations would manage the difficult tasks of nation-building and getting along with each other was a crucial question that remained to be answered.

CHAPTER TWO

THE RUSSIAN FEDERATION

More than 150 years ago a Russian historian named Mikhail Pogodin proudly proclaimed that his country was so huge and contained so much that it was not just another country, but "a whole world."[1]

While Pogodin obviously exaggerated, Russia's size and the variety of people who lived within its borders did make it unique among the nations of the world.

With the collapse of the Soviet Union in 1991, Russia lost almost 2 million square miles (5 million square kilometers) of territory. Yet it remains by far the largest country in the world. Its area is 6.6 million square miles (17 million square kilometers). Russia still stretches from the Baltic coast in Europe to the Pacific shores of Asia and crosses eleven time zones along the way. It is still farther from Moscow to Russia's easternmost territory on the Bering Sea than it is from Moscow to Washington, D.C. Russia's European territory is almost seven times larger than the second-largest European nation (Ukraine), while its Asian territory is more than one-third larger than the second-largest Asian nation (China).

A much greater difference between Russia and the former Soviet Union exists in terms of population. Russia has a population of approximately 150 million, only about half that of the former Soviet Union. However, ethnic Russians accounted for barely half the total Soviet population, and that percentage had been declining. In their smaller but still vast current territory, Russians account for about 82 percent of the population. Of the numerous minority groups, the largest are the Tatars, who make up 3.6 percent of the population. Other relatively large minority groups include Ukrainians, Belarusians, Jews, Chuvash, Chechens, Kazakhs, and Uzbeks. There are also dozens of smaller groups.

At the same time, not all Russians live in the Russian Federation. In December 1991, about 25 million Russians lived in the non-Russian republics of the former Soviet Union, although as many as 1.5 million of them had immigrated to Russia by 1996. How these people are treated is a major concern of the leaders of the Russian Federation. In any event, the presence of so many Russians in the new non-Russian countries of the former Soviet Union has created potentially explosive questions about the current borders between Russia and those countries.

Despite its vast open spaces and millions of square miles of territory in Asia, the Russian Federation is basically a European and urban country. The great majority of its people, about 78 percent, live in the European part of the country. Three quarters live in cities and large towns.

Russia's largest city is Moscow. The former capital of the Soviet Union, Moscow is home to almost 9 million people and today is the capital of the Russian Federation. Russia's second-largest city, with more than 5 million people, is St. Petersburg. Other major cities are Nizhny Novgorod, the Urals communities of Yekaterinburg and Chelyabinsk, and the Siberian towns of Novosibirsk and Omsk. Each of these cities has a population of more than one million. The largest city in Russia's Far Eastern region is Vladivostok (population about 648,000), the Siberian port whose name in Russian means "lord of the east."

Notwithstanding its losses, Russia retains many valuable natural resources. It has enormous deposits of iron, coal, oil, and natural gas. However, two thirds of Russia's oil and natural-gas deposits are in Siberia, which means they are far from Russia's major population centers and are difficult to extract because of Siberia's severe climate. Russia also still has the great taiga forests of Siberia, the largest in the world, and large supplies of gold, platinum, copper, zinc, lead, tin, and several rare metals. The picture is less favorable in agriculture, where much of the best farmland in the former Soviet Union, the so-called black earth, is located in what today is Ukraine. Yet Russia still has large areas of rich black soil in the North Caucasus region (the home of Mikhail Gorbachev), and in a broad belt of territory stretching from the Ukrainian border eastward past the Volga River and slightly beyond the Ural Mountains.

POLITICAL AND ECONOMIC PROBLEMS

When the Soviet Union collapsed, the government that the Russian Federation inherited was a malfunctioning machine made up of incompatible parts. Some were old institutions that belonged to the Communist dictatorship as it existed before the reforms of the Gorbachev era; others were relatively new, but they had been set up hastily and without much planning in the final two years of the Soviet era. In addition, under the Soviet regime the Russian people had no opportunity to learn how to live in a democracy. Suddenly, in 1991, a newly independent Russia was expected to manage the largest territory in the world, one that was riddled with an unending list of economic, social, environmental, and ethnic problems.

The Russian Federation's political system was headed by a president, Boris Yeltsin. He was elected just before the Soviet regime fell, thereby becoming the first freely elected leader in Russia's 1,100-year history. Russia's parliament, known as the

Congress of Deputies, was established and elected earlier, in 1990. (The 1,040-member Congress elected a smaller 248-member body called the Supreme Soviet to serve as Russia's day-to-day legislature.) Because the parliament was elected when the Communist Party still had a grip on power, it was controlled by supporters of the old order. In addition, the division of authority between the president and the parliament was not clearly defined. As a result, the president and the parliament struggled for power against each other, leaving Russia as a whole without an effective government at a time when one was desperately needed. Matters were not clarified by Russia's constitution, which dated from 1978. Despite hundreds of amendments introduced during the Gorbachev period, it remained in essence a relic of the Communist era and was useless as a framework for a workable democratic government.

The constitution also left unclear the relationship between Russia's central government and its regions. At its birth the Russian Federation included twenty-one major ethnic subdivisions known as "republics" that dated from the Soviet era. During the Soviet regime, most of these ethnic subdivisions inside what was then the Russian Soviet Federated Socialist Republic (RSFSR) were called "autonomous republics." However, in fact they were tightly controlled from Moscow through the local Communist Party organization. With the collapse of the Soviet Union that situation changed drastically. The ethnic republics inside the newly independent Russian Federation took advantage of the confusion and instability that accompanied its birth to assert their power and demand genuine autonomy. These demands went furthest in Chechnya, a republic in the North Caucasus region, where they eventually led to a disastrous military confrontation.

One major change as Russia began its post-Soviet era was that the Communist Party, which had ruled the Soviet Union for more than seventy years, was declared illegal. Yeltsin banned the party and ordered its property confiscated immediately after the August 1991 coup. In mid-1992, some of the Communist Party's old loyalists challenged Yeltsin's action in Russia's Constitutional Court, a branch of government established in July 1991. On November 30, the court upheld Yeltsin's ban against the Communist Party. However, it also ruled that former party members could form new communist parties. Several groups did so immediately.

Yeltsin actually put post–Soviet Russia's first government together in November 1991, while the Soviet Union officially still was in existence. One key member was Foreign Minister Andrei Kozyrev, who strongly favored a foreign policy stressing cooperation with the United States and the countries of Western Europe. Another important official was Yegor Gaidar, the deputy prime minister whose main responsibility was the critical task of economic reform. Significantly, two powerful politicians who stood with Yeltsin during the August coup were excluded from the president's inner circle: Alexander Rutskoi, Russia's vice president, and Ruslan Khasbulatov, the chairman of the Supreme Soviet.

If the breakup of the Soviet Union left Russia with a malfunctioning government, it also left its economy in a shambles. Two reasons stand out. First, for seven decades the Soviet Union devoted enormous resources to its military, but provided few consumer goods for its civilian population. As a result, many of Russia's most advanced factories produced nothing that ordinary people actually use in their daily lives.

The second reason for Russia's economic troubles is that the economy of the former Soviet Union was controlled by the state. Factories received their supplies according to government plans and in turn manufactured their products according to those plans. Almost everything was bought and sold according to prices the state set, prices that often had nothing to do with what something cost to produce. In agriculture, farmers worked on state-controlled farms where there were no incentives for extra effort. Workers in factories also labored without incentives. The unsurprising result was that most people did not work very hard. As a saying went, "They pretend to pay; we pretend to work." The entire system was wasteful and inefficient, and eventually its failures contributed to the collapse of the Soviet Union.

By the time the Soviet Union did collapse, production had declined in industry and agriculture. Inflation was high and still rising. Visitors to Moscow and other major cities were shocked to find Russians standing in the streets selling their belongings just to get money to buy food. The shelves of government stores, including food stores, often were bare, and what was available could be found only outside government channels, often illegally, at prices far beyond what ordinary citizens could afford.

The goal of the new Russian government under Boris Yeltsin was to move to a free-market system as quickly as possible. Private farmers would take over the land, and state factories and stores would be sold to private investors. This process got off to a rocky start. The Russian economy was huge, Russians had little experience with private enterprise, and powerful interests, including members of the Russian parliament, opposed Yeltsin's policies. Another difficulty was that free-market economies, although more efficient than socialist economies, often also are characterized by unemployment, bankruptcies, and prices that at times can rise very quickly. These were prospects that many Russian consumers feared and wanted to avoid.

ENVIRONMENTAL AND HEALTH PROBLEMS

Perhaps the most devastating and long-term problems the Russian Federation inherited from the defunct Soviet Union were the damage to its environment and the health of its people. The most famous Soviet environmental disaster was the 1986 explosion of the Chernobyl nuclear plant in what today is Ukraine. That explosion had its most severe impact on Ukraine, where it took place, and on neighboring Belarus, where winds carried much of the radioactive contamination. Some parts of the Russian Federation close to the Ukrainian border also were gravely affected. In the district most severely hit by radioactive fallout, at least 70 percent of the children suffered from medical problems after the Chernobyl explosion.

Unfortunately, Chernobyl was only one of many environmental disasters plaguing the Russian Federation that can be traced to Soviet policies. Large areas around the Ural Mountains are poisoned by nuclear wastes. Some of the problems date from an explosion of a nuclear waste dump in 1957, a disaster covered up for more than twenty years. As a result of that single incident, more than 11,000 people were evacuated from their homes and farming was banned over an area of 400 square miles (1,035 square kilometers). Those precautions were not nearly enough, however, as the explosion poisoned an area of 8,900 square miles (2,350 square kilometers) and exposed 250,000 people to high levels of radiation. Elsewhere in the Urals, a lake polluted by at least ten years of nuclear waste partially evaporated in 1967. Winds then blew radioactive dust over an area inhabited by more than 40,000 people, none of whom were told what was happening to them. In 1990, the radioactivity along parts of the lake shore was enough to fatally poison a person within sixty minutes. When Boris Yeltsin visited the region in June 1991, he had little but sympathy to offer the people:

> They have been concealing the truth about this radiation pollution from the people for thirty years. There has been silence. How many people have suffered? I hope that we know better now.[2]

Less than a year after that visit to the Urals, another explosion, this one at a nuclear processing plant in Siberia, spread nuclear radiation over an area of 46 square miles (119 square kilometers). Russian experts considered that accident comparatively minor.

Water pollution by industrial and agricultural wastes has received less attention than the more spectacular examples of nuclear pollution, but it is far more widespread. The waterway that is the symbol of Russia is the Volga River, where the fabled Volga boatmen long toiled. Unfortunately, each year under the Soviet regime about one fourth of all Soviet wastewater poured into the Volga. At one point along its route from the hills around Moscow to the Caspian Sea, more than 70 percent of recent fish catches were infested with worms. In one year, 1988, there were eighty-eight incidents of mass deaths of fish populations. Nor did the damage stop where the Volga ends. Pollutants have also severely damaged the Caspian Sea's sturgeon, the fish that produces Russia's world-famous caviar. Farther west, the waters of Lake Ladoga, the largest freshwater lake in Europe, have been polluted by factories near its shores. Despite partially successful efforts to protect the shores of Lake Baikal, new industries continue to foul its waters. In fact, all of Russia's major rivers are polluted, and one quarter of its drinking water is considered unsafe for human consumption.

Other environmental damage includes widespread soil erosion and deforestation, damage from acid rain, and air pollution. About 35 million Russians live in cities with polluted air. Not surprisingly, environmental damage, especially when combined with the recent economic hardship, noticeably undermined the health of the Russian people. For example, in 1992, Russia's first post-Soviet year, the number of births in the Russian Federation declined by 11 percent and the number of deaths rose by 5 percent. Serious diseases increased, among them cases of diphtheria and syphilis, both of which approximately doubled. Tuberculosis rates climbed by 11 percent. Perhaps most distressing for parents as well as most dangerous for the Federation's future, only one quarter of the country's schoolchildren were in good health.

YELTSIN VERSUS THE CONGRESS OF PEOPLE'S DEPUTIES, 1992–1993

In 1992, Yeltsin and his team forged ahead with a program of radical economic reform. Their far-reaching program was labeled "shock therapy," very unfortunate from a public-relations point of view because the term emphasized the hardships many people were experiencing. On January 2, 1992, Yeltsin ended price controls on most goods. In order to protect low-income people, exceptions were made for necessities such as milk, bread, medicines, public transport, and vodka. In addition, oil and gas prices were allowed to rise significantly but were not completely freed. At the end of the month Yeltsin lifted all restrictions on private trading. As a result, for the first time in more than sixty years, all Russians could legally be in the business of buying and selling.

Thousands of Russians responded to the new opportunities by setting up small stands known as kiosks on the streets of Russia's cities and towns. They sold mostly imported consumer goods such as liquors, canned goods, and cigarettes, generally at prices ordinary workers could not afford. More goods were available, and consumers who could afford them had greater choices.

For millions of ordinary Russians, however, the negative effects of uncontrolled prices outweighed the positive ones. During 1992, prices rose by 2,000 percent. Unemployment began to spread as businesses of all kinds tried to cut costs. Savings accumulated over many years were wiped out by soaring inflation. Overall, the Russian economy continued to shrink as both industrial production and national income fell. Not surprisingly, the number of poor people increased. By 1993, over one third of the people were classified as living below the poverty line.

The second part of Yeltsin's economic program was called privatization. It did not get off the ground until late in 1992. The goal was to transfer more than 200,000 state-owned enterprises—from small shops to gigantic factories—to private hands. Vouchers were distributed to each of Russia's citizens. They could be used to buy shares in businesses that were being privatized, either on an individual basis or by joining investment companies, or sold for their cash value. Yeltsin promised that his program would create in Russia "millions of owners, not a small group of millionaires," thereby providing the basis for a democratic society.[3]

As with price reform, privatization produced both positive and negative results. By December 1993, 77 percent of retail trade was in private hands. Progress was slower in agriculture. By 1994, Russia had 270,000 private farmers, up from only 5,000 in 1990, but they farmed only 6 percent of the land, and many were having a hard time surviving. Far more disturbing, well-placed members of Russia's old ruling elite used their connections to gain control of many of the country's most valuable enterprises and natural resources. They then often sold off these assets, becoming instant millionaires while ordinary Russians were losing their jobs.

The reaction to shock therapy was not long in coming. It came from Yeltsin's opponents in parliament, who ranged from people in the center of the political spectrum to Communists on one extreme and neofascists on the other. Khasbulatov and Rutskoi, who during 1992 moved closer to the president's hardline adversaries, became the two key leaders among Yeltsin's parliamentary opponents. Yeltsin emerged from a clash in December 1992 with his powers intact, but had to bow to parliamentary pressure and add several moderates to his government. The most important was Viktor Chernomyrdin, a former Soviet official who replaced Yegor Gaidar as prime minister. Another drawn-out struggle led to a referendum in April 1993 on Yeltsin and his economic policies; once again the president dodged the bullet by winning a majority for both himself and his economic policies.

Yet the deadlock continued, and in fact grew worse as the gap between Yeltsin and parliament widened. Matters finally came to a head in September when Yeltsin, declaring that parliament was making reform impossible, dissolved it and called for new elections. Parliament, refusing to leave its headquarters (known as the White House), responded by voting to remove Yeltsin from office and swearing in Rutskoi as Russia's new president. On October 2, stone-throwing Rutskoi supporters battled police in the center of Moscow. It was clear that an attempt to overthrow Yeltsin was under way. The president declared a state of emergency on October 3, and on October 4, Russian army troops stormed the White House and brought the anti-Yeltsin coup to an end. Official reports put the casualties at 150 dead and more than 600 wounded in the abortive revolt.

Yeltsin quickly moved to consolidate his power. He announced elections for a new two-house parliament called the Federal Assembly. The lower house, the State Duma, would have 450 seats. Half of its members would be elected from single-seat districts and half according to proportional representation, with each competing party that won at least 5 percent of the vote getting seats according to its percentage of the vote. The upper house—the Federation Council—would have 178 members, two from each of Russia's 89 territorial divisions. Yeltsin also announced that in December the people would vote on a new constitution prepared by his staff that gave enormous power to the president at the expense of the parliament.

Although Yeltsin had Rutskoi and Khasbulatov in prison, the president's opponents did surprisingly well. The leading vote-getter in the proportional representation race was an extreme nationalist group called the Liberal Democratic party. It was led by a neofascist and vicious anti-Semite named Vladimir Zhirinovsky. Another strong performer was the reorganized Communist Party led by a former Soviet-era official named Gennadi Zyuganov. Taken together, Yeltsin's opponents on the extreme left and right won about 43 percent of the vote. Reformist parties generally supporting the president took only 34 percent of the vote. The leading reformist group was Gaidar's Russia's Choice, which by virtue of its victories in single-seat districts had the largest contingent of any party in parliament. Yeltsin's main election victory was winning approval of the constitution, which strengthened both the president's powers versus parliament and that of the central government versus Russia's regions.

FROM ELECTION TO ELECTION

Yeltsin's new powers were not enough to solve his many problems. The new parliament was no more cooperative than the old one, especially in the wake of continued economic hardship and decline. Yeltsin also was unable to cope with his country's mounting crime wave, and especially with the growth of organized crime. Thousands of criminal gangs—which the Russians referred to collectively as the Mafia—not only made the streets unsafe, but controlled a large part of the private economy.

Meanwhile, a new crisis emerged in the tiny republic of Chechnya in the Caucasus region. Led by a reckless and ruthless former Soviet army officer named Djohar Dudaev, the largely Muslim republic of about 1.3 million people declared its independence. The tension grew until December 1994, when Yeltsin sent the Russian army into Chechnya to crush the independence movement. After months of bloody fighting, Russian troops seized Grozny, Chechnya's capital, and its other main towns. However, the death toll reached the tens of thousands and guerrilla war continued. Matters were made worse when Chechen gunmen in mid-1995 and early 1996 crossed the border into neighboring parts of Russia in hostage-taking raids that led to hundreds of deaths.

In December 1995, Russia once again held parliamentary elections, and this time the opponents of economic reform ran even more strongly than in 1993. The Communist Party under Zyuganov emerged as the strongest party in parliament, followed by Zhirinovsky's Liberal Democrats. The country's two strongest reform parties—Prime Minister Chernomyrdin's newly formed Our Home Is Russia and a group called Yabloko, led by economist Grigory Yavlinsky, trailed by a large margin.

The 1995 elections pushed Yeltsin further from the policies he had first followed. In January 1996, he replaced his pro-Western foreign minister Andrei Kozyrev, who had been criticized by the same forces opposed to Yeltsin's economic policies, with Yevgeny Primakov, a veteran Soviet-era official. A few weeks later Yeltsin appointed Vladimir V. Kadannikov as deputy prime minister in charge of the economy. Kadannikov immediately called for a change in policy that would rein in Yeltsin's free-enterprise reforms.

By early 1996, with the presidential elections barely a half year away, Yeltsin was highly unpopular and trailed badly in the polls compared to Communist leader Zyuganov. However, Yeltsin reorganized his campaign staff, made lavish promises to the Russian public, and used his presidential powers to deliver long-delayed services to various parts of the country. He also succeeded in making the election a referendum on communism, telling the public that, if he lost, Zyuganov would turn back the clock toward dictatorship. Zyuganov made it easier for Yeltsin with his increasingly hard-line statements during the campaign. After narrowly finishing ahead of Zyuganov in the first round of elections, but without receiving the majority required to be declared the winner, Yeltsin revamped his government. He fired several leading conservatives closely associated with the disastrous Chechnya campaign, including Defense Minister Pavel Grachev and chief of security Aleksandr Korzhakov. At the same time, he appointed former general Aleksandr Lebed, who finished a strong third in the first round, as the head of Russia's Security Council. At Lebed's urging, General Igor Rodionov was appointed defense minister. Bolstered by these steps, Yeltsin was elected decisively in the July 3 runoff with 54 percent of the vote. He immediately reappointed Chernomyrdin as prime minister. Yeltsin also appointed liberal reformer Anatoly Chubais, whom he had dismissed from the cabinet in January, as his chief of staff.

With the election won, the leading personalities in Yeltsin's government—Chernomyrdin, Lebed, and Chubais— immediately began to jockey for position and influence. Lebed, for one, made no secret of his presidential ambitions. The internal struggles in the government were especially significant in light of Yeltsin's fragile health, which clearly suffered from the exhausting campaign.

Yeltsin was inaugurated for his second term on August 9, 1996. The inauguration took place in the Kremlin Palace, a Soviet-era structure, under a double eagle, once the symbol of tsarist Russia. While both the palace and the eagle recalled Russia's powerful past, Yeltsin's shaky appearance during the ceremony was testimony to his own poor health and his country's current weakness.

Russia's weakness was disastrously demonstrated in Chechnya just before the inauguration when Chechen rebel forces dealt the demoralized Russian army a stunning defeat by seizing control of Grozny. Yeltsin then turned to Aleksandr Lebed, his recently appointed security chief, to save what he could for Russia in Chechnya. Lebed met with Chechen rebel leaders, and on August 31 the negotiators signed a cease-fire agreement. The agreement, called the Khasavyurt Accords after the village in which they were signed, was vague on several points, but there was no doubt that it amounted to a severe defeat for Russia. It called for the withdrawal of Russian troops from Chechnya and a five-year transition period,

*This 1996 photograph shows a once busy street
in Grozny, the capital of Chechnya.*

after which the people of Chechnya would decide the final status of the republic.

On signing the agreement, Lebed announced: "The war is finished, enough of it." However, the agreement was widely criticized in Moscow by politicians from many factions, and received virtually no support from either President Yeltsin or Prime Minister Chernomyrdin. Moscow's determination to keep Chechnya within the Russian Federation and an equal determination on the part of the Chechen leadership to achieve independence promised serious problems in the future. The signing of a peace treaty in May 1997 by Yeltsin and Chechnya's newly elected president Aslan Maskhadov only papered over the deep division regarding Chechnya's final status. The Chechen victory also raised concerns about Islamic Fundamentalism. Leaders in Moscow feared its influence would spread and threaten Russian control of other parts of the North Caucasus region.

Meanwhile, during the first four months of his new term Yeltsin's health, undermined by heart disease, declined to the point where he was rarely seen in public.

Yeltsin received a heart bypass operation in November. The operation was performed in Moscow by Russian doctors. However, the presence of American physicians on the scene was testimony both to what many felt was the poor health of Russia's medical system and the view in Washington of Yeltsin's importance to the future stability of Russian politics.

Back in Moscow, Lebed continued to feud with Chernomyrdin, presidential chief of staff Anatoly Chubais, and other leading figures in the Yeltsin government. Suddenly, on October 17, Yeltsin fired Lebed from all his posts. He had been in office only four months. Lebed was accused of plotting a coup, a charge he vigorously denied and for which there was little evidence. All that was certain was that at the time of his dismissal Lebed was Russia's most popular politician, the only leader in Moscow the Chechens trusted, and a formidable potential candidate for the presidency should anything happen to the fragile Boris Yeltsin.

After his surgery, Yeltsin took a few weeks to recuperate and returned to work in December, but his presence did little to end the government's paralysis. In fact, Yeltsin was still very weak and he almost immediately fell ill with pneumonia. Over the next few months he ignored repeated calls, especially from his political opponents, that he step down. Not until March 1997 did his strength return. Yeltsin then launched a new effort to revitalize his government and reform program. He began by appointing Anatoly Chubais, a staunch advocate of free-market economics, to the post of first deputy prime minister. About a week later Yeltsin announced a major governmental shake-up. He fired several ministers, eliminated some ministries altogether, and brought a new group of economic reformers into his cabinet. The most important new face at the top was Boris Nemtsov, the thirty-seven-year-old governor of the Nizhny Novgorod region, whose track record on economic reform was among the best in Russia. Two months later in May, the newly-installed reformers won a victory when Yeltsin dismissed defense minister Rodionov for failing to prepare for a smaller, less expensive military. Taken together, Yeltsin's aggressive new steps were significant. Whether they were enough to make a difference remained to be seen.

RUSSIA AND THE WORLD

While juggling its many problems at home, the Yeltsin government also struggled to formulate a post-Soviet foreign policy for Russia. Russians were divided about how to deal with the fourteen other newly independent states of the former Soviet Union, which they referred to as the "Near Abroad." Many Russians across the political spectrum found it especially difficult to accept the independence of Ukraine and Belarus, as well as the loss of the parts of Kazakhstan where Russians were the majority of the population.

One of Yeltsin's most urgent foreign-policy problems was what to do about nuclear weapons left in the territories of Ukraine, Belarus, and Kazakhstan when the Soviet Union collapsed. These weapons stood in the way of nuclear arms-reduction agreements agreed to by the Soviet Union and the United States in 1991 (START I) and Russia and the United States in January 1993 (START II). After complicated negotiations that included the United States, Ukraine, Belarus, and Kazakhstan agreed to give up all their nuclear weapons and not to acquire new ones. All three countries ratified START I as well as a second document, the Nuclear Non-Proliferation Treaty, which is designed to stop the spread of nuclear weapons.

These agreements did not prevent problems between Russia and Ukraine on other issues. One source of tension was the Crimean Peninsula, which was part of Ukraine but overwhelmingly Russian in population. The two countries also disagreed about how to divide the warships of the former Soviet Union's Black Sea fleet.

Meanwhile, beginning in 1992 the Yeltsin government faced constant criticism from both Communist and nationalist forces for its pro-Western policies. Of course, Russia's pro-Western orientation helped it to get considerable foreign aid. During Russia's first year on its own, Yeltsin's government received about $8 billion in direct aid from the United States and the other major Western powers. Russia also was admitted to the International Monetary Fund, which would enable it to borrow additional funds for economic development in the future. However, after 1993, pressure at home forced Yeltsin to harden Russia's attitude toward the West and ultimately to remove his pro-Western foreign minister in 1996.

One answer Yeltsin had for his critics was a series of agreements with Belarus, Kazakhstan, and Kyrgyzstan. On March 29, 1996 the leaders of those three states and Russia agreed to further economic and humanitarian ties. Just three days later, Yeltsin and President Aleksandr Lukashenko of Belarus created what the two men called a "Community of Sovereign Republics" (SSR). A year later, in May 1997, the two men signed a document called the Charter of the Russia-Belarus Union. While the agreements between Russia and Belarus fell far short of creating a single state, they were a strong indication that Russia had begun the process of reincorporating Belarus.

While many people can't afford basic goods, this new mall behind Red Square in Moscow caters to the wealthy new elite in Russia.

RUSSIA FACES THE FUTURE

Overall, Russia's first post-Soviet years brought very mixed news. There was considerable economic change. By mid-1995, more than 100,000 enterprises were privatized and more than one million new businesses established. The streets of Russia's major cities sported new shops, restaurants, and renovated buildings. More than two thirds of the labor force worked in the private sector. Yet the process of change was wrenching and hard. By 1995 the economy as a whole had declined by at least 40 percent, and industrial production was about half that of 1990. The harvest was the worst in more than a decade. The best that could be said was that the long slide appeared to be tapering off. But it was not over. Russia's economy declined by 6 percent in 1996, and unemployment probably was about 10 million.

In the political arena, Russia, for the first time in its history, had a freely elected president and parliament. These were accomplishments that only ten years earlier would have seemed absolutely impossible in any foreseeable future. There was also a signed agreement with NATO (North Atlantic Treaty Organization) as of May 1997 which gave Russia a limited voice in NATO affairs in exchange for NATO's expansion in Poland, Hungary and the Czech Republic. Yet the continued strength of both communist and extreme nationalist forces against a background of economic hardship, growing crime, and a variety of social problems raised serious doubts about the ability of democracy to take root in Russia. Perhaps the best evaluation of the uncertain situation came from the newspaper *Izvestia*, whose headline after Yeltsin's reelection read, "Democracy Won. Now What?"

CHAPTER THREE

UKRAINE

The moment Ukraine established its independence in December 1991, its 230,000 square miles (595,700 square kilometers) of territory made it the second largest nation in Europe, trailing only Russia. Ukraine's population of 52 million is the sixth largest in Europe. With 18 percent of the population of the former Soviet Union, Ukraine is the second most populous of the newly independent former Soviet republics, again trailing only Russia. At the moment of its birth, Ukraine even had a seat in the United Nations, the ironic legacy of a Western concession to Stalin in 1945 that gave the Soviet Union three votes in the General Assembly: one for the Soviet Union, and one each for the supposedly "independent" countries of Ukraine and Belorussia (Belarus). Its 700,000-man military force (since reduced to 500,000, with plans to cut it further) was the second largest in Europe, half again as large as the German military, and larger than the combined forces of Britain and France. And because weapons belonging to the former Soviet Union remained in place where the defunct Soviet government had located them, Ukraine in 1991 was also a major nuclear power.

Yet Ukraine was relatively unknown to its European neighbors or to the United States because, despite its size, population, and bounty of natural resources, it had been controlled for centuries by foreign powers. After the collapse of Kievian Rus in the thirteenth century, Ukraine enjoyed only two short periods of perilous and hotly contested independence, both of which were quickly snuffed out. In its tormented history, no century has been worse for Ukraine than the twentieth. As Milan Kundera, a Czech writer whose own country has known more than its share of suffering, sadly commented: "Over the past five decades forty million Ukrainians have been quietly vanishing from the world without the world paying heed."[1]

THE GEOGRAPHY AND PEOPLE

Ukraine is located on the North European Plain, just east of the Carpathian Mountains and north of the Black Sea and the Sea of Azov. About three quarters of the country is a lowland less than 200 feet (60 meters) above sea level. A large plateau with elevations between 200 and 500 feet (60 and 150 meters) occupies the western quarter of Ukraine. The only exceptions to these modest elevations are areas in the Carpathian Mountains to the west and some hills on the southeast coast of the Crimean Peninsula along the Black Sea. Ukraine's main waterway is the Dnieper River. It divides the country approximately in half—the "Right Bank" to the west and the "Left Bank" to the east—as it meanders from Ukraine's northern frontier southward to the Black Sea. Along the banks of the Dnieper is Kiev (Kyiv in Ukrainian), the capital and largest city of Ukraine.

Ukraine borders on Moldova, Hungary, Slovakia, and Poland in the west. Directly north is Belarus. To the northeast and east looms Russia. Across the Black Sea is Turkey, for centuries an enemy of the Ukrainians and Russians alike, and its largest city, Istanbul, which for about 1,600 years was called Constantinople. Before its conquest by the Muslim Turks in 1453, Constantinople was the center and capital of

This photograph was taken in the village of Poljany, Ukraine, and shows the Carpathian Mountains in the background.

the ancient Byzantine Empire. It was from the Byzantines and Constantinople that the Ukrainians' East Slavic ancestors received the foundations of their Christian Orthodox culture more than a thousand years ago.

Ukraine is extremely rich in natural resources. Often called the "bread basket of Europe," Ukraine produces large quantities of corn and grain, as well as vegetables, soybeans, sugar beets, tobacco, beef, and eggs. Its underground resources include extensive deposits of iron and coal as well as manganese, titanium, graphite, and other valuable minerals. Ukraine also has modest reserves of oil and natural gas, but not enough to meet its needs. As it did during the Soviet era, Ukraine depends on Russia for more than 90 percent of its oil and about 80 percent of its natural gas.

Its resources made Ukraine a natural site for industry during the Soviet era. Ukraine produced a large percentage of the Soviet Union's steel, electrical products, metallurgical equipment, cars and trucks, washing machines, refrigerators, and a host of other products. It also was the site of about half of the Soviet Union's nuclear plants—including Chernobyl which exploded in 1986—as well as major arms factories and space industries. Overall, Ukraine produced about 21 percent of the Soviet Union's agricultural output, about 20 percent of its industrial output, and about 25 percent of its total gross national product. A vital part of the Russian Empire before 1917, it later became even more important to the Soviet Union.

Although the majority of the people of Ukraine are ethnic Ukrainians, the country is also home to a variety of ethnic groups that are usually, but not always, distinguished by the language they speak. Thirty-eight million people, about 73 percent of the population, are considered Ukrainian, although more than 10 percent of them prefer to speak Russian rather than Ukrainian. About 22 percent of the population is Russian, the result of centuries of control by tsarist Russia and then the Russian-dominated Soviet Union. Jews—who might speak Ukrainian, Russian, or Yiddish— and Belarusians each make up about 1 percent of the population. Smaller populations of Moldovans, Poles, Bulgarians, Romanians, Hungarians, Greeks, and Crimean Tatars constitute most of the remaining 3 percent of the population.

The population of Ukraine is divided in another way: according to how conquest affected different parts of the country. The extreme western part of the country, including the industrial and commercial city of Lviv (formerly Lvov), remained out of tsarist Russian hands longer than the rest of Ukraine, and was not annexed to the Soviet Union until after

World War II. Unlike most Ukrainians, who are Eastern Orthodox, western Ukrainians belong to a branch of Roman Catholicism called the Uniate Church. In terms of culture and attitude, western Ukrainians look toward Central Europe rather than toward Russia. It was the western Ukrainians who in the late 1980s first raised the issue of independence from Soviet or Russian control.

On the other hand, the eastern and southern sections of Ukraine have the largest Russian populations. Russians are also concentrated in Ukraine's largest cities, including its capital Kiev, the port city of Odessa, and the industrial center of Kharkiv (formerly Kharkov). In these cities even the Ukrainian population tends to speak Russian.

Another subgroup of Ukrainians are the Cossacks. They are the descendants of runaway serfs whose communities managed to maintain a degree of autonomy during the sixteenth to eighteenth centuries and who still retain their distinct identity today. There is one additional major group of Ukrainians: those living in other states of the former Soviet Union. They number about six million, and most of them live in Russia, where they account for about 3.5 percent of the population.

UKRAINE'S TROUBLED HISTORY

The Ukrainian people, like the Russians and Belarusians, trace their history to the East Slavs and Kievian Rus. However, after Kievian Rus was destroyed by the Mongol invasion of the thirteenth century, Ukraine was carved up by three powers. Although in the west the principality of Galicia-Volhynia maintained its independence for a time, most of today's Ukrainian territory, including Volhynia, eventually fell to Lithuania, which was expanding southeastward from its original core near the Baltic Sea. Poland took Galicia, while Ukraine's eastern fringes became part of the Golden Horde, the state that the Mongols set up on the steppe east of the Black Sea. As power shifted over the next two centuries, the division of Ukraine changed somewhat. Most of Ukraine became part of a unified Polish-Lithuanian state, while its Black Sea coast was seized by a new power in the region: the Ottoman Empire. By the sixteenth century, several pieces of the eastern Ukraine belonged to yet another new and growing power, the principality of Muscovy.

It is this history of being torn at by the great powers that surrounded it that gave Ukraine its name, which means "borderland" in both Russian and Ukrainian. In the mid-seventeenth century, a rebellion against Poland led by a Cossack chieftain named Bogdan Khmelnytsky swept Ukraine. Thousands of Ukrainian peasants rallied to Khmelnytsky's banner, and he succeeded in defeating the Poles. However, this struggle for independence had a dark and ugly side. As they fought the Poles, Khmelnytsky's forces also turned their fury against the region's Jewish population. They murdered about 100,000 people, one of the worst massacres of Jews in history prior to the Holocaust committed by Nazi Germany in the twentieth century.

By the time the period the Ukrainians call the "Ruin" was over, the country was divided among the Russians, Poles, and Ottomans. Gradually the Russian Empire expanded at the expense of the weakening Poles and Ottomans, until it had conquered virtually all of Ukraine by the end of the eighteenth century. Only its western fringe, which was seized by the Austrian Empire, escaped Russian control.

The next important development in Ukrainian history centered around language rather than politics. Modern Ukrainian emerged from several dialects spoken in the region in the fifteenth and sixteenth centuries. The language had an oral tradition of epic poems, folk songs, and folktales. A literary tradition also emerged, consisting largely of works by Ukrainian Orthodox clergy that often were anti-Polish. However, the first great writer of the modern Ukrainian language was Taras

Shevchenko (1814–1861). His poems depict Ukrainian rural life and express the poet's love for his native land. Because he advocated Ukrainian independence, Shevchenko was sent into Siberian exile. After his death the tsarist regime intensified its policy of Russification, which included banning Ukrainian-language publications and theatrical productions. However, it was unable to stop the growing nationalist movement, as historians, writers, and poets followed Shevchenko's lead.

In March 1917, for the first time in nearly three centuries, Ukraine received a second chance at independence when the tsarist empire collapsed. At first a council called the Rada asked only for autonomy, but it proclaimed Ukraine's independence when the Bolsheviks seized power. Ukraine again became a battleground, as Bolsheviks, anti-Bolsheviks, and several Ukrainian nationalist factions fought for supremacy. Once again the turmoil left Ukraine divided and under foreign control. By the end of the civil war in 1921, most of Ukraine had been conquered by Bolshevik forces. However, a large swath in the west was in Polish hands, and a few bits and pieces were part of Czechoslovakia and Romania.

UKRAINE UNDER SOVIET RULE

Soviet rule was a catastrophe for Ukraine, as it was for every other state of the former Soviet Union, including Russia. As was the case in the other Soviet republics, the first seven years after the civil war offered a chance for recovery. The Soviet regime in Moscow permitted the Ukrainians to speak and write their language, which led to a genuine cultural revival. Ukrainian peasants were allowed to run their own farms under a moderate program called the New Economic Policy. But bad times lay ahead. In the Biblical story of Joseph in Egypt, seven good years are followed by seven bad years. In the Ukraine in the twentieth century, seven good years were followed by almost sixty bad years.

By 1928, Joseph Stalin was consolidating his personal dictatorship. Supported by Communist Party zealots who were determined to build a new socialist order and prepared to destroy anything that stood in their way, Stalin launched his program of rapid industrialization and collectivization of agriculture. Ukrainian peasants bitterly resisted collectivization, but to no avail. Huge numbers of them were shot or arrested and deported to slave labor camps. At least five million more peasants died in the 1932–1933 famine that accompanied collectivization when the Soviet regime seized most of the food from the farms and left the peasants to starve. Stalin's purges of the 1930s, when millions of people were murdered outright or sent to be worked to death in Soviet slave-labor camps, dealt yet another blow to Ukraine.

The next disaster to hit Ukraine was World War II. The German invasion of the Soviet Union brought massive suffering. The death toll in Ukraine was about six million, of whom one million were Jews murdered as part of the organized Nazi campaign to exterminate the Jewish people. An additional two million Ukrainians were drafted to work as slave laborers for the Nazis. Hundreds of thousands of Ukrainians fought the Nazis as members of the Soviet Red Army and as guerrillas. At the same time, there were Ukrainians who helped the Nazis round up and murder their Jewish neighbors or served as concentration camp guards. In two days and nights in September 1941, 35,000 Jews were shot to death, a pace of murder that not even the Nazis' extermination camps could match. Thousands of them were driven to their place of execution at the Babi Yar ravine outside Kiev through a corridor formed by Ukrainian police.

After the Germans finally were driven from Ukraine and the rest of the Soviet Union, and World War II came to an end, some Ukrainian guerrilla forces resisted the return of Soviet rule. These anti-Soviet rebels were not totally wiped out until 1949. Meanwhile, the extreme western part of

*Taken in the final bleak days of December 1941, this picture
shows survivors looking for relatives among the corpses
left by the* Einsatzgruppen, *special Nazi forces that
followed behind the advancing army with the express
mission of executing all Jews.*

Ukraine, which had been held by Poland and Czechoslovakia prior to 1939, was seized by the Soviet Union in 1945 and annexed to Ukraine. Further territorial growth came in 1954, a year after Stalin's death, when the new Soviet leader, Nikita Khrushchev, detached the Crimean Peninsula from the Russian republic and gave it to Ukraine.

Ukraine remained relatively quiet during the 1950s, but in the 1960s and 1970s both nationalist and democratic movements emerged. The Soviet regime under Leonid Brezhnev reacted with a widespread purge beginning in 1972. Although the purge was not violent, as in the Stalin years, many people lost their jobs, including Ukrainian Communist Party leader Petr Shelest. He was replaced by Vladimir Shcherbitsky, a hard-line, dictatorial bureaucrat who ran Ukraine with an iron hand for his bosses in Moscow. However, not even Shcherbitsky could crush the unrest in Ukraine. Underground publications by intellectuals and dozens of strikes by workers were proof that discontent remained beneath the surface and would not disappear.

THE GORBACHEV ERA

Although the emergence of Mikhail Gorbachev immediately brought a breath of fresh air to the stagnant atmosphere in the Kremlin in Moscow, it still took months for his policies of glasnost and perestroika to build up any steam. Glasnost, which means openness, referred to allowing the Soviet people more access to information and permitting them an expanded freedom to express themselves. Perestroika originally referred to a restructuring of the Russian economy but soon came to refer to the entire program of reform. The process was particularly slow in Ukraine, where Shcherbitsky was one of the most effective Communist Party bosses standing against reform. Most of the Brezhnev-era policies against dissidents and others who wanted to loosen the party's hold on the life of the people remained in place.

Then came Chernobyl. On April 26, 1986, an explosion tore apart one of the nuclear reactors at the Chernobyl nuclear power plant, not far from Kiev. Deadly radioactive particles were blown into the atmosphere and then began silently to rain down on the unsuspecting inhabitants near the disaster site. To the nuclear disaster was added a political one, as Soviet authorities failed to inform the people of what had happened, and in fact did not admit to the disaster until radioactivity was detected in Western Europe. Many of the heroic men who stopped the fire caused by the explosion from reaching the other nuclear reactors at Chernobyl later died from radioactive poisoning because they lacked protective clothing. It took days before people living near the extreme danger zone finally were evacuated. The Soviet government was humiliated both by the explosion and by its failure to respond appropriately.

The Chernobyl disaster had two immediate consequences. It spurred Gorbachev to increase the pace of his reforms across the Soviet Union, and, in Ukraine, it increased unrest against Shcherbitsky's authoritarian rule. A major step took place in November 1988 with the founding of the Ukrainian People's Movement for Restructuring (Rukh). Although Rukh's stated goal was to support reform within the Soviet structure, it soon began to advocate what it vaguely called "sovereignty." Eventually it called for outright independence. By 1989, a broad movement composed of many groups demanding change had developed. It included environmentalists, religious groups, and, perhaps most importantly, well organized and militant miners in the Donbass region, who organized strikes that threatened to bring the Ukrainian economy to its knees. This agitation led to Shcherbitsky's downfall in September, but the turmoil continued. In July 1990, after local elections saw non-Communists win more than 35 percent of the seats in the Ukrainian parliament, Ukraine declared its sovereignty. Shortly thereafter, the parliament elected a former Communist leader named Leonid Kravchuk as its chairman.

During late 1990 and into 1991, Ukrainian leaders consistently opposed Gorbachev's efforts to hold the country together until the unsuccessful August coup against him shattered the last vestiges of Soviet power. On August 24, just three days after the coup against Gorbachev collapsed, the Ukrainian parliament declared the country's independence. Barely three months after that, on December 1, Ukrainian voters went to the polls and voted overwhelmingly for independence, effectively destroying Gorbachev's last desperate attempt to preserve the Soviet Union. On the same day, the voters chose Leonid Kravchuk to be the new republic's first president. On December 31, the Soviet Union was dissolved, making Ukraine's independence an established fact.

Twice before—in the mid-seventeenth and early twentieth centuries—Ukraine had reached for independence. But both attempts occurred during raging storms of rebellion and war, and when those winds of war finally died down, Ukraine found itself once again under foreign control. In 1991, whatever other troubles it faced, Ukraine was at peace, and its neighbors, particularly Russia, were in no position to challenge its independence.

INDEPENDENT UKRAINE

Ukraine began the first era of independence in its history beset by many problems. Soviet policies that emphasized industrial growth over all else had made the country an environmental disaster area. Many of Ukraine's rivers, including the Dnieper, are polluted by industrial wastes and radioactive materials. The air in many cities is heavily polluted by industrial waste from chemical and metallurgical factories. Uranium mining has given the country some of the highest cancer rates in the world. Erosion and the overuse of chemicals have ruined millions of acres of farmland. And always there will be Chernobyl. In 1989 a young mother from a farming village near Chernobyl spoke to a reporter about how pollution was ruining her life and the lives of her children. Although she was speaking about her own village, her poignant words applied to millions of people throughout Ukraine whose health was endangered by environmental pollution:

> I was raised [on this land], it reared my children. And we eat virtually everything that is produced on it because it is impossible to obtain anything else.... So we eat everything that the earth produces, even though it has been contaminated.... I have four children and they are all sick. Commission after commission visits here, but to no avail. My heart bursts with grief when I see the sick children. We are hostages. We have no opportunity to leave, yet it is impossible to live here.[2]

Seventy years of Soviet communism also left much of Ukraine's population without conveniences that are considered necessities in the industrialized world. Perhaps worst off were the villages and farms, where about one third of the people live. Rural areas were ignored or exploited for many years while the Soviets focused on industrial development. As Ukraine began its independent life, only one third of its villages had medical facilities, and most of those were minimal. Most lacked even the most basic cultural facilities, such as a hall where movies could be shown. The majority of Ukraine's villages lacked running water, and only 5 percent were linked to gas lines.

In addition, as elsewhere in the former Soviet Union, Ukraine had no tradition of democratic government. Its president, Leonid Kravchuk, was a former Communist Party leader who managed to overhaul his political identity and suddenly emerge as a newborn Ukrainian nationalist just as the Soviet Union was collapsing. As president, Kravchuk initially maintained his popularity by stressing his determination to strengthen Ukraine and ensure its independence from

A typical home in Ukraine

Russia. The disputes with Russia over Ukraine's nuclear arms, the Crimea, and the former Soviet Union's Black Sea naval fleet bolstered Kravchuk's popularity, but did little to make life better for the average citizen. In November 1992, to further separate his country from its giant neighbor, Kravchuk replaced the Russian ruble with a new Ukrainian currency, another step that met with popular approval.

However, Kravchuk took few steps toward real economic reform; in particular, he did not move Ukraine toward building a free-enterprise system. He often responded to those who disagreed with him with threats, like the Soviet official he once was, rather than like the democratic president he was supposed to be. One member of parliament summed up his concern about the president's priorities, which focused on Ukrainian independence at the expense of almost everything else:

We reject the notion that one must concentrate on first building the state, and that democracy is of secondary importance. With that attitude, God knows what kind of state—authoritarian, even fascist—we may end up with.[3]

Meanwhile, in the wake of Kravchuk's inaction, the Ukrainian economy continued the decline that began during the Gorbachev era. Between 1990 and 1994, economic output dropped by 50 percent. Ukraine's new currency, introduced in late 1991, was eroded by inflation that peaked in 1993 at an annual rate of 4,735 percent. That year coal miners in the Donbass region in the eastern part of the country, many of whom were ethnic Russians, were on strike. Ordinary people found it increasingly difficult to pay for basic food necessities. As one economist put it: "It would not be an exaggeration to call the situation catastrophic. Those who call it a crisis are dangerous optimists." [4]

Ukraine also was plagued by ethnic conflicts that threatened its unity. The most dangerous situation was in Crimea, an autonomous republic where the overwhelming majority of the population was ethnic Russian and where sentiment for secession from Ukraine and reunion with Russia was strong. In January 1994, Crimean voters elected separatist Yury Meshkov as their republic's president. This began a tug-of-war between Crimea's Russian community and the central government in Kiev that lasted until March 1995, when the Ukrainian parliament abolished Crimea's constitution and dissolved its post of president.

Despite its many problems, in March 1994, Ukraine held elections to its 450-member parliament, called the Supreme Rada. The leading vote-getter was the reorganized Ukrainian Communist Party, which won about a third of the seats. Although they voted for a party that opposed market reforms in March, in July Ukrainian voters chose Leonid Kuchma, a committed economic reformer, as president over Kravchuk.

His program of economic reform, which included privatization of state-owned businesses, immediately caused tension with the Rada and its strong Communist bloc. Nonetheless, in late 1994, Kuchma was able to mobilize enough public support to get the Rada to go along with his economic program. The Rada also voted him new powers to carry out his reforms. In addition, Kuchma took the lead in persuading the Rada to approve the nuclear Non-Proliferation Treaty (NPT), under which Ukraine agreed not to acquire nuclear arms. The NPT was the last of the treaties that Ukraine had to approve to clear the way for further United States-Russian nuclear–arms reductions.

Kuchma began implementing his economic reform program in 1995. He was helped with aid from several international organizations, including the International Monetary Fund. At the same time, Kuchma appeared to change his position regarding Russia. During the election campaign he supported closer ties with Russia, and was elected on the strength of strong support from Ukraine's ethnic Russian community. By 1995, however, he was speaking about "Ukraine's return to Europe" and stressing that he did not intend for Ukraine to become "a vassal of Russia." [5]

During 1996, Ukraine took some important steps forward. Early in June the government announced that it had shipped the last of Ukraine's nuclear warheads to Russia for destruction there. At a ceremony at a missile base now empty of weapons, officials from Ukraine, Russia, and the United States scattered sunflower seeds to mark the region's return to growing life-sustaining crops instead of housing instruments of death. At the end of the month the Supreme Rada, after months of opposition from Communist lawmakers, finally adopted Ukraine's first post-Soviet constitution.

Ukraine was the last country of the former Soviet Union to adopt a new constitution. The document contained several compromises. It provides for a strong presidency, as President

Kuchma demanded, but also for a single-chamber legislature, which Kuchma's opponents in parliament wanted. Ukrainian is the official state language, but minorities such as Russians and Crimean Tatars have the right to use and be educated in their own languages. On some issues, such as the right to own private property, Ukraine's new constitution is vague, and when it was adopted parts were not even written down. Yet its adoption was a major step toward making Ukraine what Kuchma called a "predictable country." In September, Ukraine's economy became more predictable when the government introduced a new currency, the *hryvna*. It replaced the currency introduced shortly after independence, which had been severely devalued by five years of inflation.

Ukraine is a country with great potential that remains beset by instability. During 1996 its prime minister, Pavlo Lazarenko, barely escaped death in an assassination attempt when a remote-controlled bomb exploded near his car. The challenge ahead is to make independence work to better the lives for the majority of the Ukrainian people.

CHAPTER FOUR

BELARUS
AND MOLDOVA

BELARUS

Prior to December 1991, Belarus never enjoyed a day of genuine independence. Two facts about Belarus tell a great deal about the country's history and problems. First, while the name *Belarus* means "White Russia," nobody knows for certain how or why the term came to be applied to that particular region and that group of people. The origin of the name Belarus has been buried and lost under centuries of historical events, just as the Belarusians themselves throughout their history have been overshadowed and blocked from view by more powerful neighbors. Second, Minsk, the capital of Belarus, was first mentioned in the eleventh century as a town on the route from Poland to Russia. After that, Belarus often served as a highway not only for traders but also for invaders. This left its people exposed to the rampages of foreign armies and, once the fighting was over, to domination by one or more foreign powers.

Belarus occupies about 80,000 square miles (207,200 square kilometers) on the North European Plain. It is wedged between Poland to the west, Lithuania and Latvia to the northwest, Ukraine to the south, and Russia to the east.

Belarus is a lowland country covered by forests, swamps, lakes, and marshes; its highest point is only 350 feet (107 meters) above sea level. The country has few valuable natural resources aside from forests, which cover 30 percent of its territory, and large deposits of peat. Its main crops are rye, oats, wheat, potatoes, sugar beets, flax, and hemp. Its most important industrial products are machinery, motor vehicles, television sets and other electrical equipment, chemicals, and textiles. Industry and construction employ about 40 percent of the labor force and agriculture and forestry about 22 percent. About 16 percent of the Belarusian labor force work in health, science, and education.

The population of Belarus is slightly more than 10 million, 78 percent of whom are Belarusians. Russians are the largest minority group, accounting for about 13 percent of the population. The other large minority groups are Poles (4 percent), Ukrainians (almost 3 percent), and Jews (about 1 percent). Since independence, Belarus has been more successful than most other former Soviet republics in preventing ethnic conflict from flaring out of control. About 70 percent of the Belarusian population is Eastern Orthodox in religion, while about 20 percent are Roman Catholic.

The East Slavs, from whom the Belarusians are descended, have lived in the area since the seventh century; the Belarusians have seen foreign rulers come and go. After the Mongols destroyed Kievian Rus, Lithuania gradually conquered what today is Belarus. When Lithuania merged with Poland in 1569, Polish influence grew in Belarus, as did the strength of the Catholic Church. Many Belarusian nobles converted to Catholicism and began to speak Polish. Overall, Catholics are concentrated in the western part of Belarus closest to Poland, while Orthodoxy is strongest in the east near Russia. By the seventeenth century the Poles were being challenged both in Ukraine and in Belarus by the growing power of Russia. When Poland was partitioned in the late-eighteenth century by Russia, Prussia, and Austria, Belarus became part of the Russian Empire.

Just as the Poles had tried to Polanize Belarus, the Russian tsars tried to Russify the country. One tsar, Nicholas I (1825–1853), even banned the use of the name Belarus and required that the region be called "western Russia." Later tsars prohibited publications in the Belarusian language and banned its use in the schools. Meanwhile, the beleaguered country continued to be a battleground. Napoleon marched through Belarus when he invaded Russia in 1812, and huge German and Russian armies collided in battle there during World War I.

The Belarusian sense of nationality developed very slowly. The job of forging a national identity usually requires an educated elite, but until the twentieth century most Belarusians were uneducated peasants. Educational opportunities existed in the cities, but even until the end of the nineteenth century most of the urban population was Russian, Polish, or Jewish. However, some Belarusians were receiving an education, and beginning in the mid-nineteenth century they began to formulate the idea of a Belarusian nation. One of them was Kastus Kalinowski (1838–1864), who in 1863 joined with a Polish-led rebellion against Russian rule. As he awaited execution after the rebellion was brutally put down, Kalinowski left a message for future generations of his people: "For I say to you from beneath the gallows, my People, that only then will you live happily, when no Muscovite remains over you."[1]

When the tsarist empire collapsed in March 1917, Belarusian leaders formed a semigovernmental body they called the Rada (council). Their stated goal was to have local autonomy within a democratic Russia. However, the Bolshevik Party seized power in November, and its troops occupied Minsk and dispersed the Rada. Belarus then quickly passed in succession from Russian to German to Russian to Polish hands. Its declaration of independence in March 1918 meant little as powerful outside forces once again decided the country's fate. A short war between Soviet Russia and Poland ended with Belarus being divided between the two. The Poles simply made their Belarusian territories part of their new state. On the Soviet side of the border, the people of the region became part of the Belorussian Soviet Socialist Republic.

The history of Belarus under Soviet rule paralleled that of other Soviet republics, especially Ukraine. Soviet policies during the early and middle 1920s were relatively relaxed. Peasants were allowed to farm their own land, and intellectuals were given limited freedom to promote the local language and culture. The country's first university and academy of sciences were founded. However, the 1930s brought Stalin's collectivization, which the local peasants unsuccessfully resisted, and then his terror to Belarus. World War II brought the Germans, whose brutal policies, in combination with the bitter fighting it took to drive them out of Belarus, left the country in ruins. The Germans murdered more than one million people in Belarus, including most of the country's large Jewish population. One foreign visitor described what Belarus and other parts of the western Soviet Union looked like just after the war:

> For hundreds of miles...there was not a standing or a living object to be seen. Every town was flat, every city. There were no barns. There was no machinery. There were no stations, no watertowers.... In the fields, unkempt, nobody but women, children, very old men could be seen, and these worked only with hand tools.... In the winter it was even more uncanny. Then the blanket of snow concealed what tiny vestiges of life remained.... Minsk, the great capital of Byelorussia, simply was not there—only a plain of snow, broken by meaningless hummocks.[2]

After Stalin's death in 1953, a new era began for Belarus. Economic reconstruction brought some prosperity to the country. Industry and agriculture performed better than elsewhere in the Soviet Union. As a result, Belarus was better supplied with consumer goods than most other parts of the Soviet Union. Belarus also was transformed from a rural to an urban society, with two thirds of its population living in cities by 1985. Education spread, and Belarusian party leaders were given additional authority to manage local affairs. Some of them, while carefully following the party line as laid down in Moscow, stressed their identity as Belarusians as well as their Soviet citizenship. One party leader, M. A. Masherau, sometimes spoke at public occasions in Belarusian.

However, the Belarusian national identity was weakening, not growing stronger. Masherau's public speeches actually illustrated that weakness, since he spoke poorly in what was supposed to be his native tongue. All higher education in Belarus was conducted in Russian, and when an official two-volume history of the Belorussian SSR was published in 1961, it was written in Russian. Young Belarusians knew that to get ahead they had to be fluent in Russian. The Communist regime's goal of creating one "Soviet people," which in fact meant becoming Russian, went further in Belarus than in any other Soviet republic. By the late 1970s fewer than 75 percent of ethnic Belarusians spoke Belarusian as their primary language. And the percentage of ethnic Russians in the country had grown from 8 percent to 13 percent in thirty years.

By 1985 it seemed as if the Belarusians gradually were going to become Russified and disappear. Then came Mikhail Gorbachev, perestroika, and the unraveling of the Soviet Union. As in Ukraine, perestroika began late in Belarus and was stimulated, along with nationalist attitudes, by the Chernobyl disaster.

The nuclear explosion was even more disastrous for Belarus than it was for Ukraine, because Belarus lay immediately downwind from Chernobyl. Large areas of the country were contaminated by nuclear fallout, leaving thousands of peasants to raise their crops in radioactive soil. By 1991 one district was reporting childhood thyroid cancer cases at nine times the 1986 level. Other serious diseases, including leukemia, were also increasing.

In August 1991, the coup against Gorbachev totally undermined the old Communist Party leadership in Belarus. The next month Stanislav Shushkevich, a respected moderate and the former vice-rector of Belarus State University, became the country's new leader, and the parliament changed the country's name from the Belorussian SSR to the Republic of Belarus. On December 8, in the Belarusian capital of Minsk, Shushkevich became one of the founding fathers of the CIS, along with Boris Yeltsin of Russia and Leonid Kravchuk of Ukraine. With the official dissolution of the Soviet Union on December 31, 1991, Shushkevich led Belarus into the uncertain world of independence for the first time in its history.

Independent Belarus

Unlike Ukraine, which had major conflicts with Russia during the first eighteen months the CIS was in existence, Belarus got along well with its giant neighbor, in part because anti-Russian sentiment was less intense in Belarus than in Ukraine. Belarus pleased both Russia and the United States when it agreed to give up all its nuclear weapons, both short-range and long-range. In July 1992, Belarus and Russia signed a far-reaching economic agreement, which reflected the inescapable fact that most Belarusian factories depended on orders from Russia. The agreement also called for cooperation in other areas, most importantly in military matters.

However, the process of overhauling the economy went far less smoothly. Conservatives elected to the parliament in 1990, when the Soviet Union still existed, blocked President Shushkevich's reform proposals. In February 1993 the parliament lifted the ban on the Communist Party of Belarus, which had been in effect since the collapse of the Soviet Union. A year later, in January 1994, the parliament dismissed Shushkevich and replaced him with Mechislau Grib, a former police official who favored closer economic and military ties with Russia.

Belarus adopted a new constitution in March 1994. It provided for a president elected directly by the people for a five-year term, a one-house parliament (the Supreme Council) of 260 members, and an eleven-member Constitutional Court. In July the first presidential election was held. The winner was Aleksandr Lukashenko, a politician with strong anticorruption credentials, pro-Russian sympathies, and, it turned out, dictatorial attitudes.

In April 1994, just before Lukashenko's election as president, Belarus and Russia agreed to link their economies. One reason this measure had wide popular support was that the economy of Belarus, cut off from its long-standing links with Russia, was in terrible shape. Inflation was rampant, and the Belarusian ruble had fallen in value to 18,600 to the dollar. Under the agreement, Belarus adopted Russia's ruble as its currency, and tariff barriers between the two countries were eliminated. A year later, with about 90 percent of all former Soviet enterprises remaining in state hands, Lukashenko announced a new effort to privatize the Belarusian economy. However, in practice, Lukashenko halted privatization and, during 1996, launched a bid for dictatorial powers. He cracked down on the press and his political opponents, two of whom sought political asylum in the United States. Lukashenko also began a campaign for a new constitution that would give the president enormous power over parliament. The campaign culminated in November in a referendum in which voters approved measures giving President Lukashenko sweeping powers. Although the campaign was marred by charges of extensive fraud, Lukashenko acted immediately. First he replaced the Belarus parliament with a largely powerless legislative body packed with his supporters. The next day he signed into law a new constitution that confirmed his new powers.

In February 1995 an agreement with Russia further tightened the two countries' economic union and established joint control of Belarus's borders. In May, Belarusian voters approved a law granting Russian equal standing as an official language with Belarusian. Less than a year later, in March 1996, Belarus signed a detailed agreement with Russia, Kazakhstan, and Kyrgyzstan that strengthened their mutual ties. In April 1996, Russia and Belarus signed an agreement creating a "Community of Sovereign Republics" and followed that with the Charter of Russia-Belarus Union in May 1997. These agreements in theory moved the two countries closer together. In practice, however, integration was limited as Russia remained preoccupied with other problems.

MOLDOVA

Moldova, which was called Moldavia when it was part of the Soviet Union, is the second smallest and most densely populated of the former Soviet republics. Although it is near the western shore of the Black Sea and therefore enjoys a sunny and mild climate, its territory of about 13,000 square miles (32,500 square kilometers) is landlocked. Moldova is surrounded by Ukraine to the northeast and Romania to the southwest. Its capital city is Chisinau, formerly known as Kishinev.

Moldova is a lowland country through which two major rivers flow on their route to the Black Sea: the Prut, which forms Moldova's border with Romania; and the Dniester, which flows through the eastern part of the country. Moldova's rich soil produces many different agricultural crops, from wheat and corn to tobacco and a variety of fruits. It is best known for its excellent wines and liquors.

About 64 percent of the country's population of 4.3 million people is Moldovan. However, the Moldovans in reality are Romanians, with whom they share a common history, language, and culture. Moldova has several minority ethnic

A group of Gagauz folk singers and dancers
dressed in their traditional costumes

groups, of which the Ukrainians (14 percent) and Russians (13 percent) are by far the largest and most important. In fact, the tension between the Moldovans on the one hand, and the Russians and Ukrainians on the other, threatens to tear the country apart. Another important minority group is the Gagauz (3.5 percent), who speak a Turkic language and are Orthodox Christians. Their separatist demands have added to the strain on Moldova's fragile unity. Bulgarians (2 percent) and Jews (1.5 percent) make up most of the remaining population.

Apart from a brief period of independence in the fourteenth century, and when it was part of an independent Romania after World War I and during World War II, Moldova has been under foreign rule for many centuries. By the sixteenth century the Ottoman Empire had conquered the region. Turkish control lasted until the Russian-Turkish war of 1806–1812, after which the victorious Russian Empire annexed the region, which at the time was called Bessarabia. Romania, which became fully independent in 1878, took control of Moldova in 1918. The region alternated between Soviet and Romanian control several times between 1940 and 1945, according to the twists and turns of World War II, finally ending up in Soviet hands when the war ended.

For the next forty-five years the Romanians were unable to do anything about what they called the "Bessarabia question." Yet neither they nor the Moldovans accepted Soviet control of Moldova. Meanwhile, the Soviet dictator Joseph Stalin complicated matters when he created what the Soviets called the Moldavian Soviet Socialist Republic. Stalin gave several chunks of the newly acquired land to Ukraine, and added a strip along the Dniester River populated mainly by Russians and Ukrainians to the Moldavian SSR. That step helped set the stage for some of the dangerous ethnic tensions that plague independent Moldova today.

For forty years after World War II, Soviet policy was to try to break the links between Moldova and Romania. The Soviets began by declaring that the Moldovans and Romanians were two separate nationalities. Ignoring the historical record, the Soviets claimed the region had never been part of Romania, but had been ruled by foreign powers until it was "liberated" by Russia in 1812. In addition, this time ignoring the realities of how people spoke and wrote, the Soviets claimed that Romanian and Moldovan were separate languages.

In order to turn their propaganda into reality, the Soviets blocked almost all traffic across the Moldovan-Romanian border. They forced the Moldovans to write their language in the Cyrillic script used to write Russian, instead of the traditional Latin script used to write Romanian. The Soviet authorities called this artificial new language "Moldavian." In addition, the Soviets arrested and deported thousands of people. Overall, Soviet repression in Moldavia may have killed as much as 10 percent of the population between the end of World War II in 1945 and Stalin's death in 1953.

After 1953, Soviet policies were far less brutal, but the policy of Russification continued. As elsewhere in the non-Russian Soviet republics, this meant encouraging the use of the Russian language, and especially requiring children to study it in school. As a result, by 1989 over half the ethnic Moldovans in the region spoke Russian as a second language.

Nonetheless, the failure of Russification became evident after Mikhail Gorbachev came to power and introduced his policy of glasnost. By 1988 ethnic Moldovans were demanding an end to Russification of their republic. In August 1989 the local parliament adopted a law restoring the Latin script and making Moldavian the republic's official language. Name changes (of cities, streets and other places) followed, as Communist heroes were dropped in favor of figures from Moldovan history. In June 1990 and again in May 1991, the republic's name was changed, as step-by-step the country emerged from the shadow of the weakening Soviet Union. In 1990 the Moldavian SSR became the Moldovan SSR. In 1991, "Soviet" and "Socialist" were dropped and the new country simply became the Republic of Moldova.

Not everybody in Moldova was elated by the prospect of independence from Moscow. The Russians, Ukrainians, and Gagauz, the country's largest minority nationalities, feared for their rights in an independent and highly nationalistic Moldova. These concerns led to numerous confrontations, declarations and counterdeclarations, and demonstrations and strikes. Even before the Soviet Union collapsed, both the Gagauz in their southern corner of the country and the Russians and Ukrainians living in a northeast region called the Trans-Dniester announced that they would secede from Moldova. In October 1990, a dispute between the central Moldovan government and secessionists in Trans-Dniester led to violence in which six people were killed and thirty wounded.

Moldova declared its independence on August 27, 1991, shortly after the failed anti-Gorbachev coup. It joined the CIS on December 21, after carefully stating that its membership should not interfere with its independence. The country's first president was Mircha Snegur, a former Communist Party official turned nationalist, who had been elected by parliament back in October 1990. That decision was confirmed in an election held in December 1991 in which Snegur ran unopposed.

Independent Moldova

After Moldova established its independence, the economic decline that began during the Gorbachev era continued. By 1993, real income had dropped by two thirds since 1990, and inflation had reached the disastrous rate of 30 percent per month.

Meanwhile, ethnic tensions intensified dangerously and dominated the political life in the country. The Russians, Ukrainians, and Gagauz were especially concerned when several ethnic Moldovan leaders spoke openly of unification with Romania. Immediately after independence, the Gagauz near the Prut River and the Russians and Ukrainians in the Trans-Dniester region each announced their own republics. The Trans-Dniester declaration was particularly dangerous for two reasons. First, the region contains about 900,000 people and itself has no historic ties with the rest of Moldova, having been attached to it by Stalin. Second, the Trans-Dniester region is separated from the rest of Moldova by the Dniester River, which in effect forms a natural border between the Russian and Ukrainian secessionists and the central Moldovan government in Chisinau.

Faced with the loss of one tenth of its territory and one fifth of its industry, the Moldovan authorities moved to stop the secession of Trans-Dniester. The Russians and Ukrainians resisted, and fighting broke out in May 1992 in which more than 500 people died. The secessionists held their own, largely because the Russian Fourteenth Army, a unit stationed in the region during the Soviet era, sided with them. Moldovan authorities complained about a Russian army remaining in their country. But the Russian commander, General Aleksandr Lebed, responded with a remark that could only have increased the Chisinau government's concerns about keeping Trans-Dniester a part of Moldova: "There's nothing unusual about all this. There's been a Russian army here for two hundred years."[3] A cease-fire negotiated in July 1992 brought a fragile peace to the region.

The most important question for Moldova after independence was whether to reunify with Romania, a course favored by many, but not all, ethnic Moldovans. The issue was explosive because of the region's ethnic divisions. President Snegur opposed immediate reunification, and by 1993 that option had decreasing public support. Parliamentary elections in February 1994 were won by the pro-independence Agrarian Party, which included President Snegur among its leaders. In August 1994 the country adopted a new constitution, and in October Moldova and Russia signed an agreement under which Russia would withdraw its troops from Trans-Dniester by 1997. However, Russia's refusal to act on the agreement soon turned it into a dead letter.

In mid-1995, President Snegur left the Agrarian Party and formed his own organization, the Party of Revival and Accord. The split occurred because the Agrarians opposed Snegur's economic reform program, which included privatization of state-owned enterprises. By 1995 economic conditions seemed to have stabilized, and even improved slightly. However, the political situation remained unstable. During 1996, Snegur forged an alliance with ultranationalist forces and behaved in an increasingly dictatorial fashion. This did not prevent the defeat of his reelection bid in December by reformist politician Petru Lucinschi. Meanwhile, the country's unity remains fractured, if not yet entirely broken. Suspended between larger and more powerful neighbors, Moldova has uncertain prospects for the future.

CHAPTER FIVE

THE BALTIC STATES

While the Baltic countries of Estonia, Latvia, and Lithuania are distinct in terms of culture and language, they also have much in common. They are unique among the fifteen former Soviet states in that after World War I they broke away from the Russian Empire and remained independent for two decades. That era of independence ended in 1940 when the Soviet Union annexed the three small countries. The Soviet Union moved in less than a year after its notorious 1939 agreement with Nazi Germany (the Molotov-Ribbentrop pact), in which the two totalitarian powers divided Eastern Europe. The United States and Great Britain denounced these annexations as illegal and refused to recognize them for the next fifty-one years.

Among countries of the former Soviet Union, the three Baltic states culturally are the most Western and have the highest standard of living. Traditionally the Lithuanians have been strongly influenced by Poland, while Latvia and Estonia have long-standing ties with Germany and Scandinavia. The three small states also are the most urbanized of the fourteen non-Russian republics.

The small nations that share the eastern shore of the Baltic Sea are survivors. During most of the past seven hun-

Part of 1989's dramatic human chain that crossed the Baltic states to express their solidarity in opposition to the Nazi-Soviet Pact

dred years Estonia and Latvia have been ruled by foreigners, yet have maintained their distinct identities. Only the Lithuanians, who in the fourteenth century controlled a large part of Eastern Europe, enjoyed a period of independence prior to the twentieth century. The Latvians and Lithuanians speak the world's only surviving Baltic languages, a group of languages once widely spoken in Eastern Europe that are closely related to the Slavic languages. The Finno-Ugric language spoken by the Estonians is an unusual language related only to Finnish and Hungarian.

The three Baltic countries also share a basically similar physical environment. Their portion of the Baltic coast has hundreds of miles of beautiful white beaches that have long attracted vacationers from surrounding countries. It is known as the Amber Coast because of the amber stones—actually fossilized resin millions of years old from primeval pine trees—that are scattered along the beaches. Collecting and working the amber into valuable jewelry is an old tradition in the Baltic region. Local tribes traded the amber thousands of years ago, and Baltic amber has been found far to the south in ancient Egyptian tombs.

The landscape along the eastern shore of the Baltic Sea is flat with some rolling hills away from the coast. There are many small lakes and rivers and extensive pine forests. Large boulders found scattered about the flat countryside are reminders of the power of nature. Carried south thousands of years ago by advancing glaciers, and then left behind as the glaciers retreated, the boulders are called "presents from Scandinavia." Local traditions hold that these boulders have magical powers.

The Estonians, Latvians, and Lithuanians gave the world a remarkable demonstration of their shared fate and sense of solidarity on August 23, 1989, the fiftieth anniversary of the Nazi-Soviet pact. On that day more than two million people protesting that pact and their countries' subsequent annexation by the Soviet Union formed a human chain that spanned the Baltic states. It stretched more than 300 miles (480 kilometers) from Vilnius, Lithuania's capital in the southwestern part of the country, across Latvia to Tallinn, Estonia's capital on the Gulf of Finland.

During their first period of independence between the two world wars, the Baltic states tried to renew and strengthen their political and economic ties with the West. They also tried to cooperate on a variety of issues by forming the Baltic Council in 1934. In their new period of independence, the three states have taken a similar orientation. In 1990, even before independence was secured, they signed a Baltic Economic Cooperation Agreement, and in September 1991 they established a customs union to promote free trade and unrestricted travel. A broader organization, the Council of Baltic Sea States, linked the three former Soviet states to the Scandinavian countries. All three Baltic states also joined the Conference of Security and Cooperation in Europe, linking themselves to the broader European community, and NATO's loosely defined Partnership of Peace program. They likewise belong to the United Nations and the International Monetary Fund, the latter organization a source of vitally needed loans for economic development.

EJTONIA

The Estonians have lived along the shores of the Baltic Sea for more than 5,000 years. Between the thirteenth and twentieth centuries, all or part of the country was ruled at one time or another by German crusading knights; by Denmark, Sweden, Poland; and, beginning in the early eighteenth century, by Russia.

Today Estonia covers an area of about 17,400 square miles (45 square kilometers). About 20 percent of the land is covered by forests that are the home to a variety of wildlife. Vast marshes make up about 30 percent of the country; another 10 percent consists of about 1,500 islands in the Baltic Sea and Gulf of Finland. There are also about 1,500 lakes.

Estonia has a total population of about 1.5 million, of whom slightly more than 60 percent are ethnic Estonians. The Estonians were the smallest ethnic group in the Soviet Union to have their own union republic. About 30 percent of the country's population is Russian. Ukrainians and Belarusians constitute less than 5 percent of the population. Like the Finns, to whom they are closely related, most ethnic Estonians are Lutheran Protestants.

Estonia's capital and largest city is one of the many signs of foreign influence in the country; its name, Tallinn, derives from the Estonian words for "Danish castle." Many consider Tallinn the most beautiful city in the Baltic region.

The Estonian economy is heavily industrialized, largely as a result of factories built during the Soviet era that helped give the tiny republic the highest standard of living in the Soviet Union. Estonia's Soviet-era factories produce electronics, textiles, furniture, and processed foods. Its mining industry exploits deposits of phosphates and oil shale, which is used mainly to generate electric power. Peat, which is also used to generate electricity, and forests are other important natural resources. Estonia's agricultural sector produces large quantities of dairy products and meat for export. Deep-sea fishing boats sail from Tallinn and other Estonian ports.

The mining of phosphates played an important role in Estonia's struggle for independence during the late 1980s. By then, Estonians were well aware of the damage caused to their environment by Soviet-built industries and mines. When a massive plan to exploit phosphate deposits in eastern Estonia was revealed in 1987, it provoked a huge public outcry. Estonians were determined to protect the most fertile part of their country, which also is the source of its major rivers, from the inevitable pollution that large-scale phosphate mining would bring. That protest movement united Estonians from varied walks of life, thereby contributing to the growth of a national consciousness.

Estonia became part of the Russian Empire in the early eighteenth century when Peter the Great, who coveted Estonia's ice-free ports, conquered much of the Baltic region from Sweden. Because of centuries of earlier German rule, the landowning aristocracy of Estonia was German, while the ethnic Estonians were mainly peasant serfs. Russian rule strengthened serfdom, which was not abolished until the nineteenth century. The second half of the nineteenth century witnessed economic growth and a cultural awakening that helped Estonians resist tsarist attempts to Russify them beginning in the 1880s.

After breaking away from the Russian Empire in 1918, Estonia established a democratic government that lasted until the 1930s, when it was undermined by hard times caused by the Great Depression that began in 1929. In 1934, Prime Minister Konstantin Pats led a bloodless coup and established a dictatorship. After four years democracy was restored, but time was running out for independent Estonia. Less than a year after the outbreak of World War II, the Soviet Union annexed its tiny neighbor.

Soviet rule brought oppression, arrests, and deportations. In July 1941, the German army drove the Soviets from Estonia. The country remained under Nazi control until 1944, when the Soviet Union retook the region. After World War II, the Soviet regime deported tens of thousands of Estonians, rapidly collectivized agriculture, and integrated Estonia's economy into the larger Soviet economy. Industrial development brought large-scale Russian immigration into Estonia. The Russian population increased from barely 8 percent of the total in 1934 to more than 30 percent by 1989. Russians also ultimately made up about half of the local Communist Party that controlled Estonia.

By the 1970s, many Estonians feared that their country's national identity was threatened. In October 1980 about 2,000 students demonstrated against rule from Moscow in the streets of Tartu, home of Tartu University, Estonia's oldest and most important institution of higher learning. Brutal police repression led forty leading Estonian intellectuals to sign an open protest letter to Moscow. Meanwhile, thousands of Estonians looked to the West, and especially to Finland, to reaffirm their sense of being part of Europe. Finnish television broadcasts from Helsinki, just across the narrow Gulf of Finland, gave Estonians more access to outside information than any other Soviet nationality. Despite decades of Soviet

This photograph, taken in Tallinn on Estonian National Day in 1990, shows the depth of nationalistic feeling that made independence in 1991 relatively smooth.

control, the goal remained, as one Tallinn housewife put it, "to get back to Europe where we belong."[1]

The Gorbachev era quickly led to what Estonians called their "new awakening period." One early expression of that awakening was the environmental movement that developed in opposition to Moscow's plan to expand phosphate mining. By the late 1980s, the "new awakening" had turned into an independence movement. Pro-independence groups, led by the Estonian Popular Front, won a majority of the seats in the Estonian parliamentary elections in March 1990. The new parliament then chose Edgar Savisaar, the Front's leader, as Estonia's new prime minister. Pressure for independence continued until the August 1991 coup against Gorbachev. After the coup failed, the Soviet government recognized Estonia's independence.

Immediately after independence Estonia moved ahead with economic reform. The country issued its own currency, the kroon, in June 1992. After a difficult year in which the economy declined by more than 26 percent, the economy stabilized in 1993 and started to grow in 1994. Privatization spread quickly, and foreign investment, mainly from Sweden and Finland, increased. In the political arena, Estonia adopted a new constitution in June 1992. It established a system in which the parliament elects the country's president. The country's new president, who took over when Savisaar resigned in February 1992, was Lennart Meri. Parliament elected Meri to a full four-year term in October 1992. He then appointed a twenty-eight-year-old historian named Mart Laar as prime minister. Laar immediately made it clear to his fellow Estonians that they faced difficult problems. As he told them after his selection: "The first thing to do, after forming a government, is to see how the country can survive the very harsh winter we are going to have." [2]

While political disputes led to Laar's resignation in 1994, Estonia in many respects has made a successful transition to independence and a free-market economy. It has built ties and reached important agreements with its two Baltic neighbors, with the Scandinavian nations, and with the rest of Western Europe. Estonia's most serious problems are ethnic relations, in particular the role of the large Russian minority in Estonian national life, and its relationship with Russia itself. A law enacted in July 1993 limited Estonian citizenship to people living in the country before 1940 and their descendants. This effectively turned about 90 percent of ethnic Russians, even those born in Estonia, into foreigners. This angered both Russia, which still had soldiers stationed in Estonia, and the local Russian minority. Tensions increased in mid-1993 when the people of two predominantly Russian cities voted in referenda—declared illegal by the Estonian government—in favor of local autonomy. One of those cities was Narva, Estonia's second largest, which is just a few miles from the Russian border in the northeastern part of the country, a region where Russians outnumber Estonians. (Tallinn is more than 40 percent Russian, while Kohtla-Jarve, Estonia's fourth-largest city, like Narva, is about 90 percent Russian.)

Laws passed in 1993 allowed noncitizens to vote in local municipal elections and guaranteed ethnic minorities certain cultural privileges such as their own schools. These measures eased tensions slightly, although Estonian nationalists expressed alarm when Russian-speaking candidates captured 27 of 64 seats in November elections to the Tallinn city council. Moscow finally withdrew its troops from Estonia in August 1994, but the long-term position of ethnic Russians in Estonia and Estonia's relationship with its giant neighbor to the east remain unresolved. Meanwhile, Estonian democracy continued to function as Meri won a second term as president in September 1996 in a fairly contested election.

LATVIA

The Latvians are descended from people who arrived in the Baltic region at least 2,500 years ago, and perhaps significantly earlier. Latvia first was drawn into the orbit of European civilization when it was conquered and its people enserfed by German crusading knights in the thirteenth century. German rule was followed by Polish, Swedish, and Russian rule, the Russians conquering the region from Sweden in the early eighteenth century. On several occasions during these centuries Latvia served as the unwilling battleground for its larger and more powerful neighbors. Riga, its capital, was founded in 1201 by Germans, who made it a base from which they conquered the rest of the region.

Today Latvia is a country of about 24,500 square miles (63,455 square kilometers), with a population of 2.5 million. Forests and marshlands cover about a fifth of the country. Air

Riga, the capital of Latvia, and its all-important river the Daugava. The Dom Cathedral (built in the thirteenth century) is in the foreground.

and water pollution, largely caused by Soviet-era industries, has severely damaged Latvia's environment.

Because of Russian immigration during the Soviet era, Latvians today form a narrow majority of less than 52 percent. About 34 percent of Latvia's population is Russian; Ukrainians and Belarusians account for another 8 percent. The country's major cities all have Russian majorities; in Riga, Latvia's capital, about 70 percent of the population of over 900,000 was Russian at the time of independence. Like the Estonians, the majority of ethnic Latvians belong to the Lutheran Church.

Latvia's largely industrial economy produces electronic products, minibuses and streetcars, furniture, steel, and a variety of other products. Cattle and dairy farming are the most important agricultural sectors. The economy suffered during the last years of the Soviet era and immediately after independence, declining by about 50 percent between 1990 and 1993. Riga, Latvia's principal port, lost its important role as an export point for Russian oil after the collapse of the Soviet Union. In 1993, Latvia established its own currency, the *lat*, and the economy grew slightly in 1994. However, Latvia was the slowest of the Baltic states in implementing privatization.

Latvia has existed for centuries in the shadow of Russia. After proclaiming its independence in November 1918, Latvia had to repel an invasion by Bolshevik forces in 1919 before securing Soviet recognition under the Treaty of Riga in 1920. Latvia maintained a democratic government until 1934 when Larlis Ulmanis, one of the country's founders, staged a coup and established a dictatorship that lasted until World War II. In 1940, under the terms of the Nazi-Soviet pact of 1939, the Soviet Union annexed Latvia. The usual oppression and deportations followed, with 15,000 people removed during a single night in June of 1941.

The Nazi invasion of the Soviet Union put Latvia under German control until 1944. During that period the Nazis murdered almost 90 percent of Latvia's Jewish community of 85,000 people, often with the help of local Nazi sympathizers. When the Soviets returned in 1944, they deported more than 100,000 Latvians in two deadly waves (1945–1946 and 1949) and imposed the Soviet political and economic order. Collectivization began in 1948 and was completed by 1951. During the next half century, Soviet policies turned Latvia into an industrialized and predominantly urban society. As of 1989, more than 70 percent of all Latvians were city dwellers. Among the Soviet Union's fifteen republics, only Estonia had a higher standard of living than Latvia.

By the 1970s, many Latvians were concerned that immigration and Soviet policies promoting the Russian language threatened their national identity. These concerns could finally be expressed publicly during the Gorbachev era. There were demonstrations as early as May 1985. Public opinion was galvanized in 1986 by an environmental issue: a plan to build a hydroelectric plant on Latvia's main river, the Daugava, which cuts through the heart of the country before reaching the sea at Riga. In a remarkable demonstration of both national consensus and individual courage, more than 30,000 people signed petitions protesting the dam. The project was canceled in 1987.

The year 1987 also witnessed the so-called calendar demonstrations commemorating anniversaries of Soviet crimes against Latvia such as the Nazi-Soviet pact and the post–World War II deportations. The formation of the Latvian Popular Front in 1988 brought together a number of groups resisting Soviet policies, including groups committed to Latvian independence. In August 1989, Latvians joined with Estonians and Lithuanians to form a human chain of two million people that stretched across the three republics. That event was the most dramatic protest against the 1939 Nazi-Soviet pact ever seen in the Baltic states. By then Latvia already enjoyed a significant degree of autonomy from Moscow's control. Freedom finally came officially in September 1991, when the crumbling Soviet government in Moscow recognized Latvian independence.

Since independence, Latvia has been governed according to a constitution adopted in 1922. The country has a one-house parliament, which elects the president. After elections in June 1993, the parliament chose Guntis Ulmanis as the country's president. The president is Latvia's head of state and serves for three years. The government that runs the country on a day-to-day basis is headed by the prime minister, who must have the support of a majority of the parliament. Independent Latvia's second parliamentary elections were held in the fall of 1995.

Although independent Latvia has had serious economic problems, public life has been dominated by what is called the "national question": the relationship between ethnic Latvians and Russians. The country's new citizenship law of June 1994 denied citizenship to almost all post-1940 immigrants and their descendants. That turned about 30 percent of the population, mostly Russians, into noncitizens. Since noncitizens cannot receive vouchers to buy privatized companies, land, and housing, the citizenship law will have a major economic impact along with its political effect. Another law guaranteed education only in the Latvian language and required language testing for both government and private-sector jobs. The impact of this law also will be widespread, as four fifths of all Russians living in Latvia do not know the local language.

Although the Yeltsin government in Russia reacted angrily to the citizenship law, it bowed to Western pressure and withdrew its soldiers from Latvia in August 1994. Notwithstanding this help, Western European nations were critical of the citizenship law and other measures directed at the Russian minority. The Latvian government added to the tensions by demanding the return of a border district, with its mainly Russian population, which was part of pre-1940 Latvia (although part of Russia for centuries before 1918) but shifted to Russia by Stalin in 1945.

Many Latvians argue that Soviet-era immigration and Russification policies almost turned them into a minority in their own country and in effect almost destroyed it. They are determined to make sure that Latvians once again become a solid majority in their own country. How they can do that without causing serious ethnic problems at home and dangerous tension with Russia to their east remains an unanswered question.

LITHUANIA

Lithuania is the largest Baltic state in terms of area (over 25,000 square miles, or 64,750 square kilometers) and population (3.7 million people). It is slightly less urbanized than its two neighbors to the north, with 68 percent of its population living in cities and towns. Like Estonia and Latvia, Lithuania was predominantly agricultural before 1940. Its main agricultural products are cattle, dairy products, grain, and sugar beets. The country's natural resources are limited to peat and forests. Its major industrial products are paper, plastics, synthetic fibers, chemicals, and electronics.

As in Estonia and Latvia, the transition to a market economy brought economic hardship to Lithuania. The economy declined by about half between 1990 and 1993, the year the government issued a new currency called the litas. By early 1994, annual inflation was 200 percent and unemployment reached 15 percent. A slight recovery began in 1995.

Lithuania is different from Latvia and Estonia in one very important respect: unlike their northern neighbors, the Lithuanians constitute an overwhelming 80 percent of their country's population. Russians, the largest minority, make up only 8.6 percent of the population, while Poles account for 7.7 percent. Virtually all Lithuanians belong to the Roman Catholic Church, and for hundreds of years Catholicism has played a central role in Lithuanian national feeling.

The first Lithuanian state dates from the thirteenth century, when the country was still pagan. Under the leadership of Grand Duke Gediminas and his successors in the thirteenth and fourteenth centuries, Lithuania conquered territory that made it one of the largest states in Europe. Its borders stretched from the Baltic Sea to the Black Sea and included all of Belarus and parts of Russia and Ukraine. In the mid-fourteenth century Lithuania's armies even reached the outskirts of Moscow, only to be turned back three times. Among Lithuania's great victories during this period of expansion was its defeat of the Tatars in a battle near the Black Sea in 1363.

Despite its military power, culturally Lithuania lagged behind its neighbors. In the fourteenth century, Lithuanian was not yet a written language, so all governmental documents were written in Belorussian. Meanwhile, even as Lithuania expanded, it was threatened on two sides, in the northwest by German knights and in the southeast by the Tatars. The search for an ally resulted in a loose union with Poland, sealed when Lithuania's Grand Duke Jogaila married Poland's queen in 1386. The union was a dynastic one; in other words, the same family ruled two separate states. One condition of the union was that Lithuania, the last remaining pagan country in Europe, accept Roman Catholicism. The alliance soon brought results. In 1410, a joint force of Poles and Lithuanians crushed the German knights at the decisive Battle of Tannenberg, thereby stopping German eastward expansion.

In 1569, under pressure from growing Russian power, the dynastic union was converted into a full merger. However, it was not a merger of equals. Poland dominated the union politically, economically, and culturally. The Lithuanian nobility gradually was Polonized and abandoned their native language. While the Lithuanian peasants retained their old language and culture, like peasants throughout Eastern Europe they found themselves increasingly in the grip of serfdom. In effect, Lithuania lost its independence and became part of Poland.

Ultimately, however, Poland could not preserve its independence either. Over the next two centuries the Polish state weakened, largely because of its inability to form a strong central government. In the second half of the eighteenth century the country was partitioned in three stages by its more powerful neighbors: Prussia, Austria, and Russia. In 1795, when the third partition took place, the territory that today is Lithuania became part of the Russian Empire.

While under Russian control, Lithuania was subject to Russification pressures. The Lithuanians responded with a national movement in the nineteenth century designed to preserve their culture. After World War I, Lithuania reestablished its independence, as did Poland. The two countries immediately fought over Vilnius, which Poland seized in 1920 and held until the outbreak of World War II. Lithuania had to move its capital to Kaunus, its second-largest city. Democracy survived in Lithuania only until 1926, when a coup established a dictatorial regime that lasted until the country was annexed by the Soviet Union in 1940.

To secure their rule, the Soviets began large-scale deportations of Lithuanians to labor camps before being driven from the region by the Germans in 1941. While the entire country suffered under German rule, the Nazis, helped by Lithuanian sympathizers, murdered more than 90 percent of Lithuania's prewar population of 150,000 Jews.

When the Soviets returned in 1944, there were more arrests and deportations, several hundred thousand by 1953, along with collectivization and a general Sovietization of the country. Lithuanian guerrilla resistance was more extensive than in Estonia or Latvia, but still was snuffed out by the early 1950s. After Stalin's death in 1953, conditions in Lithuania improved significantly, as they did everywhere else in the Soviet Union. Lithuanians took a special pride in the achievements of their athletes, in particular their basketball players, who led the Soviet team to a dramatic victory over the United States and to a gold medal in the 1988 Olympic Games.

Lithuanian resistance to Soviet policies, to the extent it was possible in the face of the secret police, centered in the Catholic Church. During the 1970s, tens of thousands of people openly protested Soviet religious persecution. By the 1980s, a major concern among many Lithuanians was the Soviet policy of teaching Russian to schoolchildren before they could study Lithuanian. Another important concern was environmental damage caused by Soviet industries, which was often in violation of the Soviet Union's own laws.

Mikhail Gorbachev's policy of glasnost allowed the various strains of Lithuanian dissent to grow stronger and come together. In mid-1988, several organizations united to form the political party Sajudis. It soon became the spearhead for Lithuanian efforts to achieve independence. The movement had a bold and dynamic leader, Vytautas Landsbergis. In March 1990, he was chosen as Lithuania's president by the country's newly elected parliament, defeating the Communist Party candidate, Algirdas Brazauskas.

Landsbergis immediately took up the struggle for independence. He was not intimidated by Moscow's economic pressure or its use of force in January 1991, when Soviet troops in Vilnius seized government buildings, killing 14 people and injuring 700. As Landsbergis stood his ground, the ground under the feet of Mikhail Gorbachev in Moscow was shaking. As the Soviet Union began its death throes after the August coup against Gorbachev, Lithuania declared its independence. The Soviet government recognized Lithuania's independence, along with Latvia's and Estonia's, on September 6, 1991.

Lithuania's first year of independence brought economic hardship, political tension, and international embarrassment. The embarrassment occurred almost immediately. Late in 1991 the Landsbergis government began pardoning thousands of individuals convicted by Soviet authorities as Nazi war criminals. Landsbergis insisted that the Soviet justice system had denied the defendants a fair trial. While there were few defenders of Soviet justice in democratic countries, the pardons met with intense worldwide criticism. Lithuania's Supreme Court responded by halting the process, but the controversy continued. In 1994 the country's prime minister publicly apologized for Lithuania's role in the Holocaust and followed the apology with a visit to Israel.

Meanwhile, a new electoral law was passed in mid-1992, and in October voters approved a new constitution. It provided for direct election of the president, who in turn appointed the prime minister. The parliamentary elections held at the same time yielded surprising results when the voters blamed Sajudis for their economic problems. Sajudis was defeated by the Lithuanian Democratic Labor Party (LDLP), a group led by Brazauskas and made up largely of reformist Communists who had supported Gorbachev and perestroika. In February 1993 the country's voters chose Brazauskas as Lithuania's first popularly elected president.

Lithuania did make some progress despite its difficulties. It managed to have good relations with Russia, in part because Lithuania allowed local Russians to become citizens and in part because President Brazauskas made a point of trying to work with Moscow. As a result, the last Russian troops left Lithuania in August 1993, a year before they left Latvia and Estonia. The following year Lithuania signed a treaty of friendship with Poland. Privatization moved ahead through a voucher system, and by 1995 about 85 percent of state-owned enterprises had been sold to the public.

Many problems remained. The transition to democracy was far from complete. For example, in April 1995 the Council of Europe cited Lithuania for human-rights violations, mainly for denying rights to arrested individuals and members of minority groups. Of even more concern to many people, Lithuania continued to depend on two Soviet-era nuclear plants for 45 percent of its electricity. These plants are of the same design as the Chernobyl power plant that exploded so disastrously in 1986.

CHAPTER SIX

THE TRANSCAUCASUS

For thousands of years the Transcaucasus has been a meeting place of different civilizations and a crossroads where many invaders have come and gone. Civilizations ancient and modern—pre-Islamic Iranian, Byzantine, Roman and early Christian, Islamic from both Iran and Turkey, Russian, and the modern Western—all have left their mark on its peaks and valleys. The region has been conquered or fought over by many imperial powers, among them the Persians, Romans, Mongols, Turks, and Russians. The tides and waves of history have left many ethnic groups, often deeply hostile to each other, living scrambled together in a small space.

The Transcaucasus is a region where Europe meets Asia and the Christian world meets the Islamic. As so often in the past, it remains a region beset by bitter ethnic conflicts. These conflicts have greatly complicated the difficult job of nation-building for Georgia, Armenia, and Azerbaijan, the three small countries wedged between the Black and Caspian seas.

GEORGIA

Georgia is a small country of 26,900 square miles (69,670 square kilometers) and a population of about 5.5 million. Its largest city is Tbilisi (about 1.3 million). Another important city is Sukhumi, a once beautiful resort town of about 125,000 people on the picturesque Black Sea coast that was devastated by a separatist war after Georgia regained its independence at the end of 1991. Georgia is bordered on the north and northeast by Russia, on the south by Turkey and Armenia, and on the southeast by Iran. Its western border lies along the Black Sea coast.

About 70 percent of the country's population is composed of ethnic Georgians, who are Orthodox Christians. The two largest minority groups are Russians and Armenians. However, the threat to Georgia's unity comes from three smaller minority groups: the Abkhazians in the northwest by the Black Sea, the Adzharians (who are Muslim ethnic Georgians) in the southwest along the Turkish border, and the Muslim Ossetians in a region along the Russian border called South Ossetia.

While the majority of Georgia is mountainous, there is a subtropical region along the Black Sea where tea, tobacco, citrus fruits, and the grapes that produce the country's famous wines are grown. The country also has some mineral resources and hydroelectrical potential. A variety of modern industries were built during the Soviet era that produce products such as iron and steel, chemicals, machine tools, and consumer goods. Slightly more than half of Georgia's people live in urban areas.

The Georgians have lived in the Transcaucasus since ancient times. In the first century B.C., the region was conquered by the Romans. In the fourth century A.D., the Georgians converted to Christianity. For several centuries thereafter, their lands were contested by the Byzantine and Persian empires. When Islamic conquerors arrived in the seventh century, most Georgians remained Christian. In the eleventh century, the country was united for the first time. It reached the peak of its power under its Queen Tamara in the late twelfth and early thirteenth centuries, just before the arrival of the Mongols. Later centuries saw other invaders and Georgia's decline, with the country divided between the Turkish and Persian empires. Beginning in the late eighteenth century, the expanding Russian Empire gradually conquered the region.

Russian imperial rule was a mixed blessing for Georgians. It finally gave them protection against their powerful Muslim neighbors, Turkey and Iran. Yet the Georgians bristled at Russian hostility toward their culture, language, and national traditions. This uneasy relationship with Russia remains a fundamental fact of Georgia's condition today.

After a brief period of independence (1918–1921) following the collapse of the Russian Empire, Georgia was conquered by the Soviet army and annexed to the Soviet Union. Although Stalin was a Georgian, the country suffered like the rest of the Soviet Union from the dictator's collectivization and purges. In fact, the purges may have hit Georgia harder than any other Soviet republic.

Georgian nationalist sentiments, while driven underground, survived Stalin's oppression and emerged and grew in the decades after his death. Nor could Stalin snuff out the Georgian people's zest for life. Georgians are passionate people who love food and drink and having a good time. Surrounded by powerful enemies, they have learned to wheel and deal and rely on their wits, breaking the rules when necessary to get along. During the Soviet era, illegal black-market activities and corruption of varying degrees flourished. Not even Eduard Shevardnadze, the tough, efficient, and dedicated Communist boss of Georgia from 1972 to 1985, was able to stamp them out.

Georgian nationalism grew much stronger during the Gorbachev era. The leading nationalist figure was Zviad Gamsakhurdia, a well-known dissident during the Soviet era and the son of one of Georgia's most famous novelists. His Free Georgia-Round Table party, which favored independence, swept to victory in parliamentary elections of late 1990. After being elected as the republic's president by parliament in early 1991, Gamsakhurdia won the post again in a popular election in May in which he received an overwhelming 87 percent of the vote.

In December 1991, when the Soviet Union collapsed, Gamsakhurdia became president of a newly independent Georgia. However, independence brought tragedy, not national revival, to Georgia. The country immediately was torn by bitter rivalries among its leading political factions, some of which had heavily armed militias. The most powerful of them was a group called the Mkhedrioni, or "Horsemen." It was led by Jaba Ioseliani, a charismatic former convict whose activities ranged from writing plays and novels to a wide variety of criminal activities.

Gamsakhurdia added to his difficulties by turning to dictatorial methods to cope with Georgia's problems. Armed clashes quickly broke out between government forces and militias loyal to antigovernment factions. Making matters much worse, the country immediately faced secessionist movements by several Muslim minority groups. These movements plunged Georgia into war, which Russia then exploited to force Georgia back into its sphere of influence.

The result was that Gamsakhurdia was overthrown in January 1992. Although he fled Georgia, forces loyal to him remained powerful in the west, where they waged a civil war from 1992 to 1993. Gamsakhurdia's mysterious death in December 1993—it is not certain whether he was killed or committed suicide—helped end that civil war, but did little to solve Georgia's many other difficulties.

Gamsakhurdia was succeeded by Georgia's most famous son, Eduard Shevardnadze, who had left Georgia for Moscow in 1985 to become one of the leading architects of the perestroika era. Shevardnadze returned to his native land in March 1992 and in effect became its president when he was appointed head of a State Council controlled by Gamsakhurdia opponents. In October 1992, Shevardnadze was elected Georgia's president. A parliament chosen in the same election contained about thirty parties, with none holding a majority.

Shevardnadze's most urgent concern by the summer of 1992 was a secessionist movement in the Abkhazia region, which included the city of Sukhumi. Although only about 17 percent of the region's population were ethnic Abkhazians, the separatists had Russian support. The battle for Abkhazia lasted until September 1993, cost 20,000 lives, created 250,000 refugees, and severely undermined the Georgian economy. It ended with Georgia's defeat and loss of control over Abkhazia.

Shevardnadze then bowed to reality. In October 1993 he agreed to Russia's demand that Georgia join the Commonwealth of Independent States. He also agreed to permit Russian military bases in Georgia. In return, Russian forces—along with the Mkhedrioni—helped government forces defeat the pro-Gamsakhurdia rebels in western Georgia. Russia also agreed to help mediate the Abkhazian conflict. Meanwhile, Shevardnadze and his government still faced a secessionist movement along the Russian border in the region of South Ossetia, a variety of other ethnic tensions, an economic collapse, organized crime, and armed militias not under state control.

Over the next two years, Shevardnadze struggled to pull his shattered country together. He launched a new political movement called the Citizens' Union of Georgia to broaden his political base of support. He pushed ahead with economic reforms begun back in 1992, including privatization and ending price controls. By early 1995, with help from the International Monetary Fund, the Georgian economy was beginning to recover. That March, Georgia and Russia signed a new agreement in which Georgia extended Russia's rights to military bases in return for recognition of Georgian sovereignty over Abkhazia and South Ossetia. In the spring, Shevardnadze was strong enough to begin disarming the Mkhedrioni. In August, the Supreme Council approved a new constitution that provided for a strong president, a two-house parliament, and autonomy for Abkhazia. After surviving an assassination attempt, Shevardnadze in November was reelected Georgia's president with more than 70 percent of the vote, while his Citizens' Union party triumphed in parliamentary elections.

By the end of 1995, Georgia appeared to have moved away from what Shevardnadze called the "edge of extinction."[1] But only at a price. Despite Georgia's official sovereignty over the region, Abkhazia was effectively outside the government's control. Georgia itself was a semi-independent client state of Russia. And each step forward was likely to require great skill and a good deal of luck.

ARMENIA

Armenians consider themselves the people of Ararat, the majestic mountain on which Noah's Ark supposedly came to rest after the great flood described in the Bible. It is symbolic of Armenia's troubled history that today Mount Ararat no longer lies within the country's borders. The mountain's snow-covered twin peaks are visible from Armenia, but they glint in the sunlight that falls on Turkey, the country that has long been Armenia's most bitter enemy.

Armenia is a tiny landlocked country of about 11,000 square miles (28,500 square kilometers). Like Georgia, it is a Christian country in a predominantly Muslim part of the world. The smallest of the former Soviet republics, Armenia is wedged perilously between its northern neighbor, Georgia, and three Muslim states: Azerbaijan to the east, Turkey to the west, and Iran to the south. A part of Azerbaijan called Nakhichevan, which is separated from the rest of Azerbaijan by a strip of Armenian territory, lies to Armenia's southwest. Making matters more complicated, Armenians are the majority in a region called Nagorno-Karabakh that during the

Soviet era Stalin made part of Azerbaijan. The status of that region has led to war between Armenia and Azerbaijan.

The total population of Armenia is about 3.3 million people, more than 93 percent of whom are ethnic Armenians. The Armenians are one of the world's most ancient peoples. They are first mentioned in the historical record by a Persian king in the sixth century B.C., and were known to the Greek historian Xenophon, who wrote about them in about 400 B.C. The first Armenian state was founded in 190 B.C. At its peak during the first century B.C., Armenia stretched all the way from the Caspian to the Black Sea and into Asia Minor, and even included parts of Mesopotamia and Syria. In 301 A.D., Armenia took a step that has been central to its identity to this day: It adopted Christianity as its state religion, becoming the first people in the world to do so. Armenian as a written language dates from about a hundred years later. In the sixth century, Armenia established its own church, which was independent of both Roman Catholic and the Eastern Orthodox churches. It still exists today and is called the Armenian Apostolic Church.

Despite their ancient glory, for most of their history Armenians have lived under the control of more powerful neighbors, including the Romans, Persians, Byzantines, Arabs, Turks, and Russians. Because their country is situated where predominantly Christian Europe meets the largely Muslim Middle East, Armenians often have viewed themselves as an outpost of European civilization in a hostile world. Of all their conquerors, the Armenians have suffered most at the hands of the Turks, who overran the western part of historic Armenia in the fourteenth and fifteenth centuries. The struggle between the Muslim Turks and Christian Armenians for control of that region reached a horrible conclusion in 1915, during World War I. To prevent the Armenians from aiding Russia, with whom Turkey was at war, the Turkish government launched a campaign of deportation, imprisonment, and outright murder in which 1.5 million Armenians were killed. The Armenian community in the western part of their historic homeland was wiped out. That terrible event, which Armenians call "The Genocide," has played a central role in how Armenians look at the world.

Armenia is unique among the former Soviet republics in having such a large percentage of its people scattered across the globe. Armenians began to establish communities in other countries after invasions during the Middle Ages drove thousands of them from their homeland. This created what is called the Armenian diaspora, meaning the Armenian communities outside Armenia itself. Thus, of the 4.6 million Armenians who lived in the former Soviet Union, only about two thirds lived in the Armenian SSR itself. Farther afield, more than 2 million Armenians live in the Middle East, Western Europe, and North and South America. The Armenian diaspora has always been concerned about events in Armenia proper, and emigrants around the world have rallied to its aid in times of need. For example, when a devastating earthquake struck Armenia in December 1988, killing more than 25,000 people and leaving over 500,000 homeless, Armenian communities throughout the world rallied to send the victims urgently needed help. The Armenian diaspora also helped Armenia take advantage of new opportunities. Thus, when Armenia finally became independent again after the fall of the Soviet Union, a Los Angeles businessman returned to Armenia to become its foreign minister.

Today's independent Armenia is the eastern part of historic Armenia. That region was seized from Persia by the Russian Empire in 1828. After the collapse of the Russian Empire, Armenia briefly was independent. However, Turkish expansionism by 1920 threatened Armenia's existence. That same year, when the Armenians surprised many people by not resisting a Soviet invasion, a British eyewitness explained their reasoning: "Anyhow, they [the Armenians] thought it would be better to have the Russians back and to lose their independence than to be massacred by the Turks." [2]

Armenia's history during the Soviet era followed a pattern similar to that of other Soviet republics. The 1920s were a particularly good period during which Armenia recovered from the devastation of World War I.

By the 1980s, Armenia had been transformed from a mainly rural country into one that was two-thirds urban. As the 1990s began, its industries produced chemicals, electronic products, processed foods, textiles, and processed rubber. Armenia's natural resources include copper, zinc, gold, and lead. Agriculture amounted to about 20 percent of the economy and employed about 10 percent of the work force. The main crops are grains, potatoes, sugar beets, grapes, and other fruits and vegetables. Yerevan, its capital, had grown from a town of 30,000 in 1918 to a city of 1.2 million.

Armenian nationalism became a major force during the Gorbachev era. However, the main thrust of Armenian nationalism was not directed against the Russians, but against another non-Russian minority: the Azerbaijanis, a Muslim people closely related to the Turks. The focal point of Armenian nationalism was Nagorno-Karabakh. Armenians both in Armenia proper and in Nagorno-Karabakh demanded that the region be united with Armenia. In February 1988, a demonstration took place in Yerevan that dwarfed anything yet seen in the Soviet Union. One million people—almost one third of the population of Armenia—gathered to voice their demands. However, the demonstration did not achieve its goal, as Gorbachev refused to tamper with the boundaries of the republics.

Between 1988 and the collapse of the Soviet Union in December 1991, events in Armenia revolved around its struggle with Azerbaijan over Nagorno-Karabakh. The fight for Nagorno-Karabakh began in earnest in 1988, when the Nagorno-Karabakh parliament declared its independence from Azerbaijan and the Armenian parliament voted to annex the region. In 1989, Azerbaijan—abetted by Turkey on Armenia's western flank—began blocking railroad traffic through its territory to Armenia proper and to Nagorno-Karabakh. The blockade caused great hardship as supplies of food and fuel from the outside world were reduced to a trickle. It was especially harmful because Armenia imports about 95 percent of its energy supplies. The ethnic conflict produced a two-way stream of refugees: Armenians fleeing Azerbaijan and Azerbaijanis fleeing Armenia. Inside Nagorno-Karabakh, violence escalated as ethnic militias fought each other in a civil war.

After the unsuccessful coup in August 1991 against Mikhail Gorbachev, independence for Armenia, as well as for Azerbaijan, brought only more violence. An uneasy cease-fire established in 1994 left Armenian forces in control of Nagorno-Karabakh and Azerbaizanian territory connecting the region to Armenia proper. An estimated 20,000 people died in the fighting.

Inside Armenia proper, Levon Ter-Petrosian was elected president in October 1991. Most of the country's agricultural land was privatized that same year. However, privatization of other businesses proceeded slowly. The country held its first parliamentary elections in March 1995. Ter-Petrosian's anti-communist Pan-Armenian National Movement emerged as the winner amid claims that the electoral process was marred by undemocratic practices. The voters also approved a new constitution that established a parliament (the National Assembly) with a strong president empowered to appoint government ministers subject to parliament's approval.

Meanwhile, life was hard. In part because of the blockade, Armenia's economy shrank by two thirds during 1992–1993. Although by 1994 the economy started to recover, several hundred thousand people had emigrated. In March 1995, the government began privatizing the country's largest state-controlled enterprises. Because of a desperate shortage of energy, in the fall of 1995 Armenia reactivated its Metsamor nuclear power plant, which had been shut down after the December 1988 earthquake. Western experts worried that the plant was unsafe. It is near two major geological fault lines and is similar in design to the Chernobyl plant.

Ter-Petrosian won a second term in the September 1996 presidential elections amid documented charges of fraud. He responded by having the police close down the offices of opposition parties and expelling most of their deputies from parliament.

AZERBAIJAN

The name Azerbaijan means "land of flames." The name comes from the fires fueled by methane escaping from underground oil and gas deposits, which to ancient eyes created miracles by making both rocks and the shallow waters of the Caspian Sea burn. The mythology of the region records how its ancient people worshipped the fires that sprang inexplicably from things that should not burn. Even today, the coat of arms of the city of Baku, Azerbaijan's capital on the Caspian Sea coast, carries three torches on a background of sea waves.

Today's Azerbaijanis, or Azeris, are the descendants of Turkic tribes that first came to the region in large numbers in the eleventh century. After two centuries of Mongol rule, Turkey and Persia, and later Russia, struggled for control of Azerbaijan. In the early nineteenth century, Russia and Persia split Azerbaijan between them. The northern section, which fell to Russia, is today the independent country of Azerbaijan. The Azeris speak a Turkic language but are followers of the Shi'ite version of Islam found in Iran.

Azeris make up about 83 percent of the population of Azerbaijan. Russians, who account for about 6 percent of the population, are the largest minority. Most of the country's Armenian minority has fled Azerbaijan for Armenia or the Armenian-controlled region of Nagorno-Karabakh.

*A photograph of the old section of Baku. In the middle
of the picture is a tower called the Maiden Tower.
Legend has it that a cruel ruler kept his daughter locked up
there. This section of town dates to the thirteenth century.*

Azerbaijan is a country of about 33,400 square miles
(86,500 square kilometers), with a population of 7.5 million. It
borders on Russia and Georgia in the north, Armenia in the
west, and Iran in the south. Nagorno-Karabakh is in the western part of Azerbaijan, just east of the Armenian border. The
country's westernmost region, Nakhichevan, is separated from
the rest of Azerbaijan by a strip of Armenian territory. Azerbaijan's eastern border, where Baku lies on the beak-shaped
Apsheron peninsula, is the Caspian Sea. The country produces
cotton and a variety of agricultural crops, but its main natural
resources are huge deposits of oil and natural gas. The modern

oil industry came to Azerbaijan in the 1880s, when the first foreign oil companies set up shop in Baku. By 1900, Azerbaijan's oil wealth had made Russia the world's leading oil producer, a position it soon lost to the United States.

After the Russian Empire collapsed during World War I, Azerbaijan was independent from 1918 until it was overrun by the Soviet Red Army in 1920. During the Soviet era, it suffered through collectivization and various purges like other parts of the country. Azerbaijan also suffered another indignity: Despite its great oil wealth it lagged badly behind the Soviet Union as a whole in its standard of living. This became a source of great resentment that found its expression once it became possible to speak openly after Mikhail Gorbachev began his reforms in 1985.

The Gorbachev era brought a great deal of turmoil to Azerbaijan. The struggle with Armenia over Nagorno-Karabakh began in earnest in early 1988, when the local Nagorno-Karabakh parliament declared its independence from Azerbaijan. Anti-Armenian riots in the industrial city of Sumgait northeast of Baku led to retaliation against Azeris in Armenia. Soon Baku was flooded by 200,000 Azeri refugees from Armenia. In September 1989, Azerbaijan began its blockade of all railway traffic and goods bound for Armenia. In January 1990, Azeri violence against local Armenians led to a crackdown in which Soviet troops armed with tanks killed more than 150 innocent bystanders. Meanwhile, two major factions, the local Communist Party and the newly formed nationalist Azerbaijan Popular Front (APF), struggled to win popular support. By adopting some of the nationalist slogans of the APF, the Communist Party won the parliamentary elections in the fall of 1990. A year later, the Communist candidate Ayaz Mutalibov ran unopposed in Azerbaijan's first direct, but clearly not democratic, presidential elections.

The turmoil grew worse after independence. President Mutalibov was forced to resign in March 1992 because of

Azerbaijan's military failures in Nagorno-Karabakh. After several more months of disorder, and Mutalibov's brief return to office, Ali Elchibey, the leader of the APF, emerged as the country's president in June 1992. He lasted in office for barely a year, becoming, like his predecessor, a victim of Azerbaijan's failures in Nagorno-Karabakh. On June 18, 1993, a familiar face won a parliamentary vote and became Azerbaijan's new president. He was Heydar Aliyev, who had run the country for much of the Brezhnev era. Aliyev's status was confirmed in October in another suspicious election in which he supposedly received over 98 percent of the vote.

Like Eduard Shevardnadze in Georgia, Aliyev recognized the reality of having to compromise with Russian power in the Transcaucasus. In July 1993 he agreed to return Azerbaijan to the CIS (it had left the organization in 1992). However, Russia provided no help to Azerbaijan regarding Nagorno-Karabakh. In addition, the Russians continued to dispute Azerbaijan's claims to offshore oil in the Caspian Sea. In September 1994, Azerbaijan signed a deal with ten foreign oil companies to develop Caspian Sea oil. The Russians objected, even though Russia's Lukoil company received 10 percent of the deal.

As of 1996, Azerbaijan remained in a precarious situation. Nagorno-Karabakh and territory connecting to Armenia proper was firmly in Armenian hands. Azerbaijan itself was plagued by political instability, economic chaos, and a host of other problems. It also was squeezed by pressure from its powerful neighbors: Turkey, Iran, and especially Russia. While Azerbaijan's oil wealth held the promise of a better future, there were fires to be put out before that promise could be realized.

CHAPTER JEVEN

CENTRAL
AJIA

The Russian conquest of Central Asia took more than one hundred years. It began in the mid-eighteenth century and lasted until late in the nineteenth century, making Central Asia the last region to be annexed by the Russian Empire. History repeated itself after the collapse of the empire and the establishment of the Soviet Union. Of the parts of the defunct Russian Empire that the Soviets retained after World War I, Central Asia resisted Soviet conquest the longest, in some cases into the late 1920s.

Today the five newly independent states of Central Asia—Kazakhstan, Uzbekistan, Turkmenistan, Tajikistan, and Kyrgyzstan—stretch from Turkey to China. They have much in common. With the exception of Kazakhstan, which has almost as many Russians as Kazakhs, their populations are overwhelmingly Muslim. They have the common experience of more than a century of Russian-Soviet colonial rule and mismanagement. They also are all burdened by depressed economies, damaged environments, and ethnic strife. And they lack any experience with democracy.

The states of Central Asia are divided by bitter ethnic feuds. During the Soviet era, the government in Moscow exploited these differences and followed a divide-and-rule policy. One of the most damaging policies was to draw borders that left large numbers of one ethnic group as a minority in the neighboring republic of another ethnic group. Thus the traditionally Tajik cities of Samarkand and Bukhara are in Uzbekistan, while more than a million Uzbeks live in Tajikistan. When Soviet controls began to weaken in the late 1980s, ethnic violence surged. As Central Asia emerged from a long era of Russian-Soviet control, its 60 million people faced an uphill struggle in building viable societies and nation states.

One of the most ironic aspects of that struggle is that none of the five states in the region wanted to become independent. They were forced into independence when the leaders of Russia, Ukraine, and Belarus created the CIS in December 1991.

Kazakhstan's President Nursultan Nazarbayev worked hard to preserve a reformed Soviet Union during its last years and months. The other national leaders in the region held similar views. They were all well aware how much the economies of their struggling countries depended on the Soviet Union. They also knew that their republics depended on Soviet institutions for many of their links to the outside world. In addition, Central Asia's leaders feared that border disputes would plague their republics as independent states. For example, Kyrgyzstan, Tajikistan, and Uzbekistan all have territorial claims on each other. Kazakhstan faces territorial claims from Uzbekistan, Turkmenistan, and, possibly and most dangerously, from Russia.

One major effort to bring stability to the region was the formation of the Central Asian Economic Union (CAEU) in 1993. A meeting of the presidents of Kazakhstan, Uzbekistan, and Kyrgyzstan in January 1997 was seen as an attempt to strengthen the CAEU.

Independence for a region as troubled as Central Asia also has become a problem for countries elsewhere in the world. One major concern was that these poverty-stricken nations would turn to producing drugs to solve their economic problems. And, in fact, that has happened. Within a year after independence, the cultivation of the opium poppy increased dramatically in the region. The crumbling of Soviet authority and the failure to replace it allowed drug trafficking to skyrocket. In Kazakhstan, growing the opium poppy was legalized, while the Fergana Valley, which runs through Kyrgyzstan, Tajikistan, and Uzbekistan, became a center for the growing and smuggling of drugs. Another concern in Central Asia is the spread of Islamic fundamentalism, a potentially destabilizing force.

In short, Central Asia's problems involve not only the states of the region but countries all over the world. That is one reason many nations have taken an interest in a region that so recently was virtually ignored by the international community.

KAZAKHSTAN

Kazakhstan is the giant of the non-Russian republics of the former Soviet Union. Its area of just over 1 million square miles (2.6 million square kilometers) makes it the eighth-largest country in the world. It extends eastward for 1,200 miles (1,930 kilometers) from the Volga River in Europe to the Altai Mountains in the heart of Asia, and southward for 800 miles (1,287 kilometers) from the edge of the West Siberian Plain to the deserts of Central Asia. The countryside is a mixture of lowlands, plateaus, and mountains, ranging from the sub–sea level Caspian Depression to the peaks of the Altai Mountains. Kazakhstan shares a long border with Russia to the west and north. In the east it borders on China, and in the south it abuts the former Soviet republics of Turkmenistan, Uzbekistan, and Kyrgyzstan.

Kazakhstan is rich in natural resources. Its northern farming belt, first opened to large-scale agriculture in the 1950s, produced one third of the wheat in the former Soviet Union, as well as a large amount of cotton and other agricul-

Before Russia conquered them, the Central Asian states were loosely organized in khanates. This picture from around 1896 shows a group of men in the khanate of Khiva.

tural crops. The country also is a major producer of meat. Kazakhstan also produced most of the former Soviet Union's chrome, one fifth of its coal, and large amounts of silver, lead, gold, and several other minerals.

Most important, at least for Kazakhstan's future, are its vast reserves of oil and gas. Its Caspian Sea coast contains the Tengiz oil field, one of the world's largest. The oil has attracted considerable foreign investment to the country. By the year 2010, Kazakhstan should be producing 1.6 million barrels of oil a day, which will make it a significant player among the world's oil-exporting countries.

Aside from its potential wealth, which far exceeds that of any of the other Central Asian states except Turkmenistan, Kazakhstan is unique among the former Soviet republics in that it lacks an ethnic majority in its population of about 17 million. Although the Kazakhs, with about 45 percent of the population, are the largest single group, they barely outnumber the local Russian population. Russians and Ukrainians together account for 35 and 5.5 percent of the population. Since ethnic Germans make up about 6 percent of the population, Kazakhstan's population is about half European. Other ethnic groups include the Tatars, Uighurs, and Dugans, the last group being Muslims from China who fled across the Russian border after a failed uprising in 1872 against the Chinese Empire.

Today's Kazakhs, who are mostly Sunni Muslims, are descended from nomadic Turkic and Mongol tribes who have wandered across the region for two thousand years. By the eighteenth century, the Kazakhs were grouped into three loose federations, but they faced invasions from Mongol tribes to the east. Some Kazakhs accepted protection from the expanding Russian Empire. After the Mongol threat receded, the Kazakhs resisted further Russian expansion, but they were no match for the Russian Army, which completed its conquest of Kazakhstan by the 1860s.

Russian control of Kazakhstan meant an influx of Russians and Ukrainians, about one million of whom settled in the region between 1906 and 1915. The government tried to pressure the Kazaks to give up their nomadic way of life to free farmland for the Russians and Ukrainian immigrants. But whatever injustices occurred under the tsars were dwarfed by what took place under the Soviet regime. Stalin's collectivization campaign brought utter catastrophe to Kazakhstan. As many as one million Kazakhs, one quarter of the total Kazakh population at the time, died during forced collectivization and the famine that accompanied it. Meanwhile, during the 1930s more immigrants came from the west, mainly Russian and Ukrainian peasants who had been deported from their lands for resisting collectivization. After Stalin's death, they were joined by another wave in the mid-1950s, people brought in to farm the Kazakh steppe, which was being opened up to cultivation for the first time. These settlers were concentrated in Kazakhstan's northern districts along the Russian border, where they constitute a majority of the population today. The Soviet leader placed in charge of Kazakhstan during that time was Leonid Brezhnev, who later would head the entire Soviet Union for eighteen years.

The Soviet Union did more than farming in Kazakhstan. Large new projects, including the Baikonur space center, brought industrial development, and also new Russian immigrants, to Kazakhstan. New industries also brought serious pollution. Giant lead smelters, in which workers toiled without protective masks or clothing, were among the worst offenders. Moscow's decision to turn Central Asia into the Soviet Union's main cotton-producing center took most of the water from the rivers that flowed into the Aral Sea, which lies on the Kazakhstan-Uzbekistan border. This caused the Aral Sea to begin to dry up, exposing huge salt flats from which desert winds blew salt and other poisons over thousands of square miles of land and millions of people. But the most frightening pollution came from nuclear testing sites in the eastern part of the country, which exposed millions of people to radioactive fallout. In August 1991, even before Kazakhstan became independent, its government closed the Soviet nuclear test sites near the town of Semipalatinsk.

Although all important decisions about Kazakhstan were made in Moscow by the central Communist Party leadership, after 1956 the job of carrying out those decisions was turned over to local Kazakh leaders. The man in charge for almost thirty years was Dinmukhamed Kunaev. He promoted many Kazakhs to important positions within the local Communist Party, and raised the educational level and national pride of the population. However, Kunaev was extremely corrupt, and was removed from office in 1986, a year after Mikhail Gorbachev became the Soviet leader.

Kunaev's removal from office and his replacement by a Russian produced the first violent ethnic outburst of the Gorbachev era. It took place in mid-December 1986, in the capitol, Alma Ata (today Almaty), and resulted in several deaths and at least 200 injuries. During the next three years, Kazakh nationalism grew, focusing mainly on issues such as environmental damage to the region and Russian Soviet distortions of Kazakh history. Russians and Ukrainians and smaller ethnic groups feared losing the protection they had enjoyed in earlier years. The worst incident of ethnic strife was between Kazakhs and oil workers from the Lezgin ethnic group, who originally were from the Caucasus region. That violent outburst led to a curfew that remained in effect for more than three weeks until tensions subsided.

In June 1989 an ethnic Kazakh named Nursultan Nazarbayev, reputed to be moderate and sensible, became the Communist Party chief in Kazakhstan. Nazarbayev tried to mediate between Kazakhs who wanted to assert their long-suppressed national identity and Russians and Ukrainians who feared that Kazakh nationalism would lead to discrimination against them. Nazarbayev was well aware that ethnic tension between these two groups could easily tear Kazakhstan apart. In particular, he knew that the large Russian population that had been in Kazakhstan for generations considered the region a part of Russia, especially those areas in which Russians were in the majority. For that reason, and because Kazakhstan was so closely tied to Russia economically, Nazarbayev strongly supported Mikhail Gorbachev's effort to keep the Soviet Union together. Nazarbayev was overwhelmingly elected president of Kazakhstan in February 1990, and used his popularity to support Gorbachev vigorously during the unsuccessful coup attempt of August 1991 and in the months that followed. When that failed, Nazarbayev led his country into the CIS in December. In part because of his insistence, the December 8 meeting in Minsk between the leaders of Russia, Ukraine, and Belarus that founded the CIS was followed by a second meeting in which eight other republics were recognized as CIS cofounders. That meeting took place on December 21 in Alma Ata.

Afterward President Kunaev and Kazakhstan were left alone to deal with their grave environmental, economic, and ethnic problems. More than half of the population lived below the poverty line. While little could be done in the short term about many problems, Kazakhstan's oil and other natural resources quickly attracted foreign investment. The biggest deal was a genuine blockbuster: a multibillion-dollar contract signed by the U.S.-based Chevron Oil Company in April 1993. Kunaev also won praise from the United States and other Western powers when Kazakhstan agreed to give up all its nuclear weapons and sign the nuclear nonproliferation treaty.

Ethnic problems, while not as acute or violent as in other Central Asian republics, remained Kazakhstan's immediate danger. A constitution adopted in 1993 made Kazakh the country's official language, but only required that the president be able to speak Kazakh, not that he be an ethnic Kazakh. The new constitution also was an attempt to convince Russians they had a place in an independent Kazakhstan.

Nonetheless, the exodus of Russians continued. At least 300,000 left for Russia in 1994 alone. It also remained an open question whether those Russians still in Kazakhstan—many of whom have been in the region for generations and consider it their homeland—would try to have the country's Russian majority districts secede and unite with Russia. Ethnic Germans, another highly skilled group, also joined the exodus. By 1996, more than 630,000 out of an original population of just over a million had left Kazakhstan for Germany.

During its first years of independence, Kazakhstan made little progress toward democracy. In 1993, Nazarbayev set up a new political party, the People's Unity of Kazakhstan (SNEK). It promptly won parliamentary elections the following year that were widely criticized because many opposition candidates were excluded from participating. These elections were followed in April 1995 by a referendum—in other words, Nazarbayev excluded all opponents—in which the president extended his term until the year 2000. Both that referendum and one in August, in which voters approved a new constitution, were justifiably criticized as undemocratic. The new constitution provided for a powerful president, who appoints the prime minister and other ministers, and a two-house parliament. It also guaranteed private property.

On the economic front, Kazakhstan's economy began to stabilize in 1995 after declining severely during the first years of independence. There has been some economic reform, including the lifting of price controls and a start in privatization. In 1994, Kazakhstan joined in an economic union with Uzbekistan and Kyrgyzstan.

In a move of far greater potential significance, on January 20, 1995, Kazakhstan and Russia signed an agreement calling for the unification of their respective armed forces. That agreement was yet another indication of the intrusive role Russia intends to play in the affairs of many of the states of the former Soviet Union.

UZBEKISTAN

The Uzbeks are the most numerous ethnic group in Central Asia. There are 16.5 million Uzbeks, about 14 million of whom live in Uzbekistan, where they constitute about 69 percent of the population. They were the third most numerous national-

*This unusual photograph shows a fair, ferris wheels
and all, which took place in Samarkand (now
part of Uzbekistan) sometime in the late 1890s.*

ity group in the former Soviet Union, trailing only the Russians and Ukrainians. The largest minority groups among Uzbekistan's nearly 20 million people are Russians (11 percent), followed by Tajiks, Kazakhs, and Tatars (each 4 percent).

Uzbekistan is a country of 170,000 square miles (440,000 square kilometers) located in the heart of Central Asia. It is bordered on the east and north by Kazakhstan, with which Uzbekistan shares the shrinking and polluted Aral Sea.

Turkmenistan lies to the southeast, Afghanistan directly to the south, and Tajikistan to the east. The country's major river is the Amu Darya, whose waters fed the Aral Sea before they were diverted to irrigate cotton fields. Most of Uzbekistan is arid; the country has long hot summers and short cold winters.

Tashkent, the capital, lies along the ancient Silk Road that once connected China and the West. Most of Tashkent's past glory is gone. Almost all of the old city was destroyed in a devastating earthquake in 1966, its buildings replaced by dull and poorly constructed Soviet-style structures. Two other important cities in Uzbekistan are Samarkand and Bukhara, both of which still boast many old mosques and other examples of traditional Islamic architecture.

The Uzbeks are descendants of nomadic Mongol tribes who arrived in the region in the fifteenth century and gradually mingled with local inhabitants. Like the Kazakhs, they are mainly Sunni Muslims. In fact, the Uzbeks are closely related to the Kazakhs, although, unlike the Kazakhs, the Uzbeks gave up their nomadic ways and became farmers long before the Russians arrived in Central Asia. Also unlike several other Central Asian peoples, the Uzbeks had a written language prior to the Russian conquest. One Uzbek poet, Nismaddin Alisher Navoi (1441–1501), is regarded by some as one of the world's outstanding poets in any language.

The territory that today is Uzbekistan was conquered by Russia during the 1860s and 1870s. During the Soviet era there was some industrial development in the region, but most of the workers were Slavic immigrants from the European part of the Soviet Union. The cultivation of cotton had a greater impact on Soviet rule in Uzbekistan. Cotton had been grown in the region for 2,000 years, and new varieties were introduced during the tsarist era, but the Uzbeks also grew a variety of grains, fruits, and vegetables. During the 1930s, however, cotton began to replace these crops. Orders from the

Soviet planners during the 1960s forced even greater increases in cotton production. By the 1980s, Uzbekistan was growing two thirds of the Soviet Union's cotton, almost as much as the entire United States. But Uzbekistan did not benefit from its cotton crop. After being harvested by methods that were abandoned in the United States about 1900, the cotton was sold at a low price to factories in other regions of the Soviet Union. By the end of the 1980s, more than 45 percent of the people of Uzbekistan lived below the Soviet poverty line.

Because cotton cultivation requires huge amounts of water, the major rivers that flow into the Aral Sea were exploited to irrigate the enlarged cotton fields. Enormous quantities of toxic pesticides, including many that were banned in the United States and Europe, were poured on the cotton, and on the workers toiling in the fields. Often they were children as young as ten years old, who during the harvest were brought to the fields in the morning and left to work without protection under the blazing desert sun.

The impact of these practices on the environment and on public health has been disastrous. The drying up of the Aral Sea has affected Uzbekistan more than any other Central Asian country. The pesticides and other poisons used to grow cotton have literally ruined the health of the entire nation. Cancer and other diseases are epidemic among the Uzbeks. Child mortality rates in some parts of the country are among the highest in the world. Mukhammad Salikh, an Uzbek poet and politician, has described what the cotton monoculture— the growing of cotton to the exclusion of all other crops—has done to his country:

> There is a direct link between the deteriorating ecological situation in Uzbekistan and the cotton monoculture. We have lost not only our lands and waters, we have forfeited the health of our people. The land is ailing and also the people who work on it.[1]

During most of the Soviet era, the tensions in Uzbekistan were kept under control. This changed during the Gorbachev era. Gorbachev's policy of glasnost stimulated Uzbek nationalism, and that nationalism in turn caused fear among Uzbekistan's minority populations. The tension eventually exploded in two violent outbursts between Uzbeks and minority groups. In the summer of 1989, fighting between Uzbeks and the minority Meskhetian Turks resulted in more than 100 deaths. The following year a similar clash between Uzbeks and Kyrgyz groups led to more than 200 deaths.

When Uzbekistan became independent in December 1991, two million of its citizens, most of them young people, were unemployed, and few jobs were available for a rapidly growing population. One of the few bright spots has been the discovery of oil. Uzbekistan also has large gold deposits, which accounted for one quarter of the former Soviet Union's total gold production. There are some signs that cotton growing, which is still too important to Uzbekistan's economy to give up, could be made less damaging to the land and the people. In 1992, Uzbekistan signed a contract with experts from Israel to produce cotton using Israel's unique drip irrigation method, in which water is delivered directly to plants through rubber hoses laced with tiny holes. Working on a few thousand acres, the Israelis cut water use by two thirds and used 10 to 20 percent less pesticides and fertilizers, while increasing production by 40 percent.

Democracy has bleak prospects in Uzbekistan. In the presidential elections of December 1991, a former Communist leader named Islam Karimov was the winner amid charges of fraud. In January 1992, six opponents of the new president were killed in clashes with authorities. Later that year members of an opposition political party were beaten and arrested. Since then, Uzbekistan, notwithstanding its 1992 constitution that supposedly guarantees democracy and respect for human rights, has become a dictatorship. Parliamentary elections in

December 1994 and January 1995 and a referendum three months later in which 99.6 percent of the voters "approved" extending Karimov's term until 2000, were clearly fraudulent. By then, according to the human-rights organization Freedom House, Uzbekistan was one of the world's twenty worst abusers of human rights. It joined the former Soviet states of Turkmenistan and Tajikistan on the list, as well as more well-established tyrannies such as Saudi Arabia, Iraq, Libya, Syria, China, Cuba, North Korea, and Vietnam.

Meanwhile, the Karimov regime has done a balancing act in relation to Islam. It has tried to use Islam to build national identity but also keep it within strict limits. Karimov and the former Communist Party officials around him fear the growth of extremist and fundamentalist Islamic movements beyond their control. As one Western observer put it, they view Islamic fundamentalism "as something approaching a return to the Middle Ages."[2] The government therefore banned the Islamic Revival Party and other fundamentalist groups. In economic affairs, the Karimov regime pushed reform, including privatization. Karimov also led Uzbekistan into an economic union with Kazakhstan and Kyrgyzstan. His model for the future appeared to be China, with its increasingly free-market economy and one-party dictatorial state. Whatever course he takes, many problems lie ahead. Mukhammad Salikh, the defeated candidate in the December 1991 presidential election, evaluated his country's condition as it faced its uncertain future: "We can only hope. Apart from hope, we have very little else."[3]

A slightly more optimistic evaluation, although still very cautious and resigned, came from a peanut merchant, who carefully insisted on remaining anonymous when speaking to a Western reporter:

> We know that the country is not always kind. But we can live well here if we are quiet. There is no war, no famine. If we are quiet we are left alone.[4]

TURKMENISTAN

Turkmenistan is a large country with a small population and many problems. Its territory is an arid belt about 420 miles (675 kilometers) wide that extends for 720 miles (1,160 kilometers) from the Caspian Sea to Afghanistan. It borders Kazakhstan to the north, Uzbekistan to the north and east, and Iran in the south. Turkmenistan has a severe continental climate of hot summers and cold winters. With a total area of 188,500 square miles (488,215 square kilometers), it is the fourth largest of the former Soviet states. Ashkhabat, the capital city, is located along the Iranian border midway between the Caspian Sea and the Afghan border.

Turkmenistan has significant deposits of potassium, sulfur, and sodium chloride. But by far the most important natural resources in Turkmenistan are oil and huge deposits of natural gas. Because Turkmenistan has only 3.5 million people, its valuable natural gas may provide the revenue to solve some of the massive problems the country faces.

The Turkmen make up about 72 percent of the country's population, the main minority groups being Russians (10 percent), Uzbeks (9 percent), and Kazakhs (3 percent). Although the Turkmen are the descendants of tribes that came to the Central Asian steppe about a thousand years ago, they did not emerge as a distinct group until the fifteenth century. They never formed a national state prior to Soviet rule, and their main loyalties to this day continue to be to tribe and clan, rather than to country. Nonetheless, the Turkmen fiercely resisted Russian conquest, holding out longer than any other group in Central Asia. In 1881, in their last great battle against tsarist forces, 14,500 Turkmen died in the unsuccessful defense of a fortress called Geok-Tepe. Resistance flared up again after the Bolshevik Revolution. At first the Turkmen fought alone against the Bolsheviks; then, during the 1920s, they joined a wider rebellion of Central Asian tribesmen called the Basmachi Revolt. Turkmen resistance flared again during Stalin's collectivization drive and was not completely extinguished until 1936.

Soviet rule in Turkmenistan amounted to nothing less than colonial exploitation. As in other Central Asian states, the Marxist government in Moscow, which officially was atheistic, tried to break the hold of Islam on the local population, but without success. Economic policies focused mainly on increasing cotton production and exploiting the region's gas and oil deposits. To provide water for cotton, the Soviets built the Kara-Kum canal, which took water from the Amu Darya river to cotton fields in the desert. The Kara-Kum project was the largest irrigation project in Soviet history, and one of the most disastrous. The canal helped destroy both the Amu Darya river, which a health official noted has been turned into "little more than a sewage ditch," and the Aral Sea into which the river flows.[5]

Aside from the oil and gas industries and one major chemical complex, there was little industrial development in Turkmenistan during the Soviet era. As a result, Turkmenistan is one of the least urbanized of the former Soviet republics, with about 55 percent of the population still living in the countryside. However, rural living in Turkmenistan is not healthy, mainly because of the pollution caused by cotton growing. Turkmenistan has the highest infant mortality rate and the lowest life expectancy of any former Soviet republic.

Turkmenistan is also one of the poorest former Soviet republics. According to Soviet standards, which are far lower than those in the United States, more than 58 percent of the people of Turkmenistan live in poverty. Because the country has so few industries, it has one of the highest unemployment rates among the former Soviet states. Turkmenistan's high birthrate, the second highest among those states, means that its unemployment situation is certain to get worse.

After Mikhail Gorbachev came to power, the Communist Party in Turkmenistan was able to weather the political storm of perestroika far better than did party organizations in many other Soviet republics. Turkmenistan's Communist Party controlled the country's elections to the nationwide Congress of People's Deputies in 1989, and despite newly organized opposition it also controlled elections to local offices in 1990. The party's leader, Saparmurad Niyazov, won the presidency of Turkmenistan in October 1990 in an election in which he ran unopposed, just as in the old days before Gorbachev's reforms.

With the collapse of the Soviet Union, Turkmenistan became independent. Its people immediately began to reclaim their national identity. One important step in that direction involved the Akhal-Teke horse, to many the national symbol of the Turkmen. The Akhal-Teke is a slender, delicate horse with a shimmering coat. For centuries Turkmen have bred it for beauty rather than strength or speed. According to one expert, it is the first purebred horse in history and the ancestor of the English and American Thoroughbred horse. However, the Akhal-Teke nearly became extinct during Soviet rule. It was considered useless by the officials who ruled Turkmenistan from Moscow. Since 1991, private breeders, with enthusiastic government support, have worked to increase the Akhal-Teke's numbers and restore it to its former glory.

At the same time, Turkmenistan quickly moved down the road to a new dictatorship. As in Kazakhstan and Uzbekistan, those who ran the country prior to independence held on to power after independence. Niyazov continued as president. The Communist Party remained intact, merely changing its name to the Democratic Party of Turkmenistan. Opposition parties were quickly hounded out of existence and their leaders driven into exile. A new constitution adopted in May 1992 left little power to the country's main representative body, the People's Council, or another parliamentary body called the Mejlis. A few days after the constitution was adopted, Niyazov staged a presidential election in which he

An exquisite Akhal-Teke horse

was the only candidate. In another "election" in January 1994, 99.5 percent of the voters approved conditions that in effect made Niyazov president for life. In early 1995, the president's birthday became an official national holiday.

In building his personal power base and promoting national identity, Niyazov has promoted Islam. He made the traditional Islamic pilgrimage to the holy cities of Mecca and Medina in Saudi Arabia and has financed the building of many new mosques. Another way Niyazov has strengthened his position and popularity is by using Turkmenistan's revenues from natural-gas sales to maintain the local economy and standard of living. He has moved very slowly in introducing economic reforms. Beginning in June 1993, the entire population began receiving water, gas, and electricity free of charge. Yet life has remained difficult in Turkmenistan. Most of its people live in poverty. As one melon farmer put it, "Life has always been hard in the desert, but it has gotten harder."[6] That increased hardship does not seem to bother Niyazov, who has stated that "anybody who complains about going without sausage or bread for a day is not a Turkman."[7]

Turkmenistan's economic future will depend heavily on its natural-gas riches. Plans call for building a multibillion-dollar pipeline for exporting gas through Iran and Turkey, which would give Turkmenistan an alternative to the current pipeline that runs through Russia. The country also can sell oil, cotton, horses, and carpets on the world market. Turkmenistan's small population and high earnings from its natural resources give it brighter economic prospects than other Central Asian countries. Its grim political prospects, on the other hand, darken the country's overall future considerably.

KYRGYZSTAN

Kyrgyzstan is a small mountainous country locked between Kazakhstan to the north, Uzbekistan to the west, Tajikistan to the south, and the People's Republic of China to the east. Three valleys account for most of Kyrgyzstan's lowlands: the Chu and Talas valleys near Kazakhstan, and the Fergana Valley that also runs through Tajikistan and Uzbekistan. Large sections of the lofty mountains along the Chinese border have a permanent cap of ice and snow. Kyrgyzstan's total area is about 76,600 square miles (198,400 square kilometers).

The Kyrgyz probably arrived in the region about a thousand years ago, but did not emerge as a distinct people until the sixteenth century. Their primary loyalties still are to tribe and clan, rather than to the Kyrgyz nation. Overall, the Kyrgyz account for only 52 percent of the country's population, which is about 4.3 million. Russians account for 21 percent and Uzbeks, with whom the Kyrgyz often have clashed, account for 13 percent. Smaller minorities include Ukrainians (3 percent), ethnic Germans (2 percent), and Tatars (2 percent). The largest influx of Russians occurred during the Soviet era. Most of them congregated in the cities. Even today, Russians and Ukrainians together account for the single largest percentage of Kyrgyzstan's urban population. In Bishkek, the country's capital, perhaps a quarter of the population is Kyrgyz.

The Kyrgyz did not resist Russian occupation during the 1860s and 1870s, in part because of the brutal treatment they received from the Kokand khanate, which controlled a large part of Central Asia before the Russians arrived. However, they turned against the Russians during World War I, when the tsarist government tried to draft Kyrgyz men into its army. The uprising was brutally suppressed. At least 100,000 Kyrgyz were killed out of a total population of less than 800,000.

The Kyrgyz received their own political organization for the first time in 1936 when they were placed in what was called an "autonomous region" within one of the Soviet republics. However, by then the country already was reeling from Stalin's relentless waves of repression.

In addition, Russification policies were distancing young Kyrgyz from their heritage. While some Kyrgyz resented this, in the cities many youths who were educated in Soviet-era schools admired the Russian language and culture as agents of progress. The outstanding symbol of those Kyrgyz who feel comfortable in both Kyrgyz and Russian culture is the writer Chingiz Aitmatov (born in 1928). Aitmatov's plays and short stories have been very popular throughout the former Soviet Union, and his works have been translated into many languages. In 1990, a reformist member of the Kyrgyz parliament described the difficulty of living in two cultures:

I would not have a right to call myself a son of my people without knowing the Kyrgyz language. But without a deep knowledge of Russian, I would not consider myself a complete man.[8]

This attitude may have pleased the Russians, but it placed a cultural barrier between many educated urban Kyrgyz who expect to lead their newly independent country and the large majority of ethnic Kyrgyz who still live in the countryside.

Whatever their disagreements with one another, the Kyrgyz have more serious problems with ethnic minorities. Beginning in the early 1990s, Russians began leaving the country and returning to Russia. The greatest tension, between the Kyrgyz and Uzbek communities, exploded into a week of violence in June 1990. According to official reports, more than two hundred people were killed. But unofficial reports put the death toll at more than a thousand.

In addition, after independence Kyrgyzstan had to contend with many of the crises found in other Central Asian states, including widespread poverty and unemployment, a high birthrate and rate of infant mortality, and rapid population growth. To cope with these problems, the country does have some mineral resources, fast-running rivers that provide hydroelectric energy, and some excellent land for raising farm animals. It also had a widely respected president, Aksar Akayev, a physicist who was the only non-Communist to head a newly independent Central Asian state. However, in order to run the country, Akayev had to rely on many former party members who had vital managerial and technical skills. Many of them opposed his efforts at economic reform, in particular the privatization of large state-owned enterprises.

Akayev, who became Kyrgyzstan's first popularly elected president in October 1991, had to struggle on many fronts at once after independence. The economy declined severely through 1994 as the president struggled to move the country toward a free-market system. During that period Aksayev freed most prices from state control and privatized most of the country's small businesses. The following year he brought Kyrgyzstan into an economic union with Kazakhstan and Uzbekistan. By 1995, Kyrgyzstan's economy was showing some signs of recovery. One good piece of news was an agreement with a Canadian company to develop the country's Kumtor gold field. In March 1996, Kyrgyzstan signed a twenty-eight-point agreement with Russia, Belarus, and Kazakhstan that focused mainly on strengthening economic ties between the four countries.

On the political front, a new constitution adopted in 1993 and amended in 1994 replaced the old Communist system with a two-house parliament and a popularly elected president. Parliamentary elections in February 1995 were considered reasonably fair by foreign observers.

Akayev also did what he could to stop the emigration of educated and skilled Russians and other Europeans from Kyrgyzstan, a loss he called his "main sorrow."[9] When the new constitution was written, he successfully fought provisions that the country's president be an ethnic Kyrgyz and that it observe the moral values of Islam. His efforts had some effect; by 1994 the emigration of Russians and other Europeans was slowing.

By the middle of the 1990s, Kyrgyzstan's problems remained formidable. Bringing the country's ethnic groups together into a workable relationship remained the most urgent task. Uzbekistan's claim on Kyrgyz territory and the danger that warfare in Tajikistan would spill across the border were other serious concerns. Despite a slight improvement, the economy was far from able to provide jobs for Kyrgyzstan's growing population. At the same time, Kyrgyzstan under Akayev had taken measurable steps toward democracy, a unique accomplishment in troubled Central Asia.

TAJIKISTAN

With an area of 55,300 square miles (143,227 square kilometers) Tajikistan is the smallest of the Central Asian states. It is squeezed into the southeast corner of Central Asia between Uzbekistan to the north and east, Kyrgyzstan to the northeast, China to the east, and Afghanistan to the south. The towering Pamir Mountains, sometimes called the "Roof of the World," run through Tajikistan. Among their peaks are the two highest mountains in the former Soviet Union. Less than 10 percent of Tajikistan is lowland, and more than half of it exceeds 10,000 feet (3,000 meters) above sea level. Although Tajikistan is small, it has a wide range of climates. The temperature can reach as high as 87 degrees Fahrenheit (30 degrees Celsius) in the subtropical air of its valleys during the summer and plunge to 50 degrees below zero in the thin, icy air of the mountains during the winter. Tajikistan's capital is Dushanbe.

Ethnic Tajiks make up about 62 percent of Tajikistan's population. The Tajiks have lived in Central Asia longer than any other group. They differ from the other Central Asian peoples in that they are Persian rather than Turkic. Tajik is closely related to the language spoken in Iran and parts of Afghanistan. In fact, there are as many Tajiks living across the Afghan border as there are in Tajikistan. The Tajiks, who emerged as a distinct ethnic group by the eighth century A.D., are the descendants of people who have lived in Central Asia since at least 1000 B.C., many centuries before the arrival of the Turkic peoples who dominate the region today. In fact, settlements in Central Asia from which Tajiks may trace their most ancient roots extend back to 3000 B.C.

The Russian minority in Tajikistan, which is shrinking as Russians flee the disorder of the region and return to Russia, makes up about 8 percent of the population. Because of the way Soviet dictator Joseph Stalin drew Tajikistan's bor-

A modern day street scene in Tajikistan

ders in the 1920s, about a quarter of its population is Uzbek. Stalin's borders placed the largely Uzbek city of Khozhent in Tajikistan, while leaving the old Tajik cultural centers of Samarkand and Bukhara in Uzbekistan.

Tajikistan suffered in the same way as the rest of Central Asia under Soviet rule. Tajiks played a major role in the Basmachi Revolt of the 1920s, and a few rebel forces remained active in the country until 1931. They also resisted Soviet atheistic propaganda as much as any other local ethnic group. Underground Islamic activity was reported during the 1970s, well before Soviet controls weakened in the following decade. The Soviet invasion of Afghanistan in 1979 caused great distress in Tajikistan. The Soviet regime used Tajiks to work in Afghanistan to support the local Communist government there, and Soviet Tajiks fought in the Soviet army that tried to put down an Islamic rebellion against that government. That pitted Tajiks against rebels from all of Afghanistan's ethnic groups, including Tajiks. In 1991, when it was possible to speak openly about the Afghan war, a leading Tajik reformer and intellectual named Bozor Sobir said that no Tajik should take pride in any medal he won while fighting in Afghanistan. His opinion was echoed by a Tajik soldier who said that Tajiks in Afghanistan were fighting people of the "same race, same blood, and same language."[10]

Independence from the Soviet Union has brought more tragedy than progress to Tajikistan. Immediately after the August 1991 coup against Mikhail Gorbachev, a struggle for power broke out between the Communist Party and several opposition groups, including a Muslim party that wanted to impose strict Islamic religious rule on the country and a group advocating democracy. In November the Communist Party leader, Rakhman Nabiyev, was elected in a presidential election marred by fraud. By the spring of 1992, Tajikistan was locked in a civil war. Nabiyev was forced to resign in September, and an unlikely and unstable coalition of Islamic and democratic forces held the upper hand in the country through the fall. However, those loyal to the old order counterattacked in December. By mid-1993, forces supporting the Tajik Communists once again were in control, although the situation was complicated by old clan and regional divisions. In addition, the most powerful military force in the country was a militia headed by an ex-convict named Sangak Safarov. The Tajik civil war produced horrible brutality on both sides, claimed an estimated 50,000 lives, created hundreds of thousands of refugees, and devastated the local economy. Several rounds of negotiations failed to end the periodic outbursts of fighting that continued once the main battles of the civil war were over.

In the political turmoil that accompanied the fighting, a hard-line leader of the pro-Nabiyev forces, Emomali Rakhmonov, emerged as Tajikistan's president in November 1992. He was reelected in November 1994. At that time the voters also approved a new constitution, which established a new parliament and a popularly elected president. Significantly, the main opposition parties boycotted both the 1994 presidential election and parliamentary elections in early 1995. The recurring violence during 1994 meanwhile took the lives of two deputy prime ministers.

In February 1996, Rakhmonov bowed to rebel demands and dismissed three officials accused of corruption. A few days later he appointed a carpet merchant as the country's new prime minister. The newly installed minister promised to move ahead with economic reforms. In February 1997, with his forces in control of only 20 percent of the country, Rakhmonov agreed to peace talks with one of the Islamic groups fighting his government. Other opposition groups were left out of the deal, which seemed unlikely to produce peace. Five years after independence Tajikistan's future looked as grim as its past.

MAPS AND FLAGS OF THE FORMER SOVIET UNION

Eurasia and Historical Russia

The Former Soviet Union

Fifteen Independent States

Flags of The Fifteen Independent States

OCEAN

EAST SIBERIAN SEA

LAPTEV SEA

BERING SEA

Kolyma

Lena

SEA
OF
OKHOTSK

Aldan

Angara

Amur

KIRGHIZ

MERKIT

**Genghis Khan's
territorial base**

SEA
OF
JAPAN

NAIMANS

Karakorum

GHARS

Peking

Liangchow

Ninghsia

Sian

GREAT KHAN EMPIRE

EURASIA AND
HISTORICAL
RUSSIA

IRE.

UNITED
KINGDOM

NORTH SEA

NORWEGIAN SEA

A R C T I

Svalbard

*Franz
Josef*

NORWAY

DENMARK

SWEDEN

Murmansk

BARENTS SEA

*Novaya
Zemla*

W. GER.

E. GER.

BALTIC SEA

FINLAND

Tallinn

WHITE SEA

KARA SEA

Dic

CZECH.

Riga

Leningrad

*Lake
Oneiga*

Arkangel'sk

Novyy Port

AUS.

POLAND

Vilnius

N. Dvina

Ob

S O V I E

HUN.

Minsk

Smolensk

EASTERN EURPEAN PLAIN

✧ Moscow

ROM.

Kiev

Dnieper

Gorki

WEST SIBERI
PLAIN

Ob

BUL.

Odessa

Don

URAL MOUNTAINS

Irtysh

Sverdlovsk

*Sea of
Azov*

Saratov

Kuybyshev

Chelyabinsk

BLACK SEA

Volga

Omsk

CAUSASUS MTS.

Rostov

Stalingrad

Magnetogorsk

Novosibir

TURKEY

Astrakhan

CASPIAN SEA

Aral

ARAL
SEA

KAZAKH HILLS

Lake Balkhash

T'blisi

SYRIA

Almaty

IOR.

Baku

IRAQ

Tashkent

SAUDI
ARABIA

IRAN

Samarkard

TIAN SHAN

AFGHANISTAN

**CLIMATIC
REGIONS**

PAKISTAN

INDIA

NEPAL

Tundra

Forests

Steppes

Desert

OCEAN

BERING SEA

Anadyr

EAST SIBERIAN SEA

Kolyma

KOLYMA RANGE

Korf

LAPTEV SEA

Kamchatka
Peninsula

Nordvik

Tiksi

CHERSKY RANGE

Lena

Magadan

SEA
OF
OKHOTSK

CENTRAL SIBERIAN PLATEAU

Okhotsk

arka

U N I O N

Yakutsk

Sakhalin
Island

Kuril
Islands

Tura

Mirnyy

Angara

Aldan

Aldan

Amur

Bratsk

Lake
Baikal

Khabarovsk

Krasnoyarsk

Irkutsk

Ulan Ude

Kyzyl

Vladivostok

MONGOLIA

ALTAY MOUNTAINS.

GOBI DESERT

N.
KOREA

SEA
OF
JAPAN

JAPAN

CHINA

0   1000 miles

0   1500 kilometers

IBET

THE FORMER SOVIET UNION

O C E A N

BERING SEA

EAST SIBERIAN SEA

LAPTEV SEA

Anadyr

Korf

Kolyma

*Kamchatka
Peninsuld*

Nordvik

Tiksi

Magadan

SEA
OF
OKHOTSK

Lena

Okhotsk

garka

Yakutsk

*Sakhalin
Island*

*Kuril
Islands*

Tura

Mirnyy

Aldan

Aldan

Yenisey

Angara

S   S   I   A

Amur

Khabarovsk

Bratsk

*Lake
Baikal*

Krasnoyarsk

Irkutsk   Ulan Ude

Vladivostok

SEA
OF
JAPAN

Kyzyl

MONGOLIA

N. KOREA

JAPAN

C H I N A

0   1000 miles

0   1500 kilometers

TIBET

FIFTEEN
INDEPENDENT
STATES

ESTONIA

The Greek historian Herodotus referred to the "black-cloaked" people of the North with whom Estonians associate their ancestors. Their flag thus includes black—as well as blue for fidelity and white for snow. It dates from 1881.

RUSSIA

Emperor Peter the Great chose white, blue, and red as the colors for the Russian flag, based perhaps on the red, white, and blue flag he had seen in the Netherlands. The flag was one of many modern Western ideas he picked up in his Dutch travels during 1697 and 1698.

LATVIA

In 1279 a reference was recorded about Lettish (Latvian) troops carrying a "banner red in color, cut through with a white stripe." The modern revival of that flag began in the nineteenth century when student groups used the flag in their rallies against Russian rule.

MOLDOVA

Although its language, culture, and blue, yellow, and red flag are Romanian, Moldova had been under Russian or Turkish rule for most of the past five hundred years before gaining freedom in 1991. The traditional Bessarabian coat of arms appears on the flag.

LITHUANIA

Yellow for ripening wheat, green for the forests and for hope, red for flowers and love of country—these are the colors chosen in 1918 for the new national flag of independent Lithuania to replace the old red banner with a mounted knight in white.

UKRAINE

Golden fields of grain under blue skies is the message of the Ukrainian flag established in 1918 and readopted in 1991. However, the colors go back to the thirteenth century blue shield of Galicia, which bore a gold lion. The majority of Galicia is now part of independent Ukraine.

BELARUS

The country's name means "White Russia," and its flag bears a traditional embroidery pattern on a white stripe at the hoist. Based on the Communist-era flag, the 1995 banner has green for forests and fields, red for "market socialism."

ARMENIA

Supposedly the first Christian nation, Armenia chose the "rainbow of Mount Ararat," which God displayed after the Flood, as the basis for its flag. Approved in 1918, the red, blue, and orange tricolor disappeared under communism but was revived in 1990.

GEORGIA

National heroine Queen Tamara (1184-1213) supposedly used a white flag with a cross and seven pointed star of dark red. These colors, combined with black as a reminder of the dark days of past foreign rule, became the Georgian flag in 1917 and again in 1990.

AZERBAIJAN

In 1917, Azeri nationalists hoisted a flag honoring their religion (a star and crescent and the color green for Islam), their Turkic ancestry (light blue), and their desire for modernization (red). It was readopted with independence in 1991.

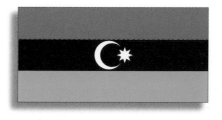

KAZAKJTAN

Light blue, a centuries-old Turkic color, stands for open skies. The eagle is for freedom. Other traditional symbols—a blazing sun and a national clothing ornament—were incorporated in the flag adopted in 1992, following independence in 1991.

KYRGYZJTAN

Manas the Noble is said the have united forty tribes to form the Kyrgyz nation under a red banner. The forty sun rays recall the tribes, while the central emblem on the sun is the roof hole of the traditional Kyrgyz home, the felt yurt.

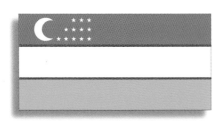

UZBEKIJTAN

The famous medieval conqueror Tamerlane (Timur the Lame) used a flag of blue, readopted in the 1991 Uzbek flag. White is for peace, green for agriculture, red for life, the crescent for the birth of a new nation, and twelve stars for the months of the year.

TAJIKIJTAN

Following independence in 1991, Tajikistan created a new flag with the same colors as its Communist-era design—red, white, and green. The gold crown stands for state sovereignty; its seven stars for the unity of intellectuals, workers and peasants.

TURKMENIJTAN

The only country in the world to feature a carpet pattern on its flag, Turkmenistan is also proud of its Muslim faith as reflected in the green background and stars and crescent. The five carpet emblems represent specific tribes.

CHRONOLOGY

OF THE POST-SOVIET STATES

1985-1991: THE END OF THE OLD ORDER

1985
- Mikhail Gorbachev named Soviet leader. Beginning of the era of *perestroika*.

1986
- Chernobyl nuclear disaster

1987
- Gorbachev fires Boris Yeltsin for criticizing the slow pace of reform.

1989
- Elections to the Congress of People's Deputies. Boris Yeltsin is among those elected.

1991
- Unsuccessful coup by Communist hard-liners against Gorbachev. Yeltsin leads the resistance to the coup.
- Soviet Union recognizes the independence of Latvia, Lithuania, and Estonia.
- Levon Ter-Petrosian elected president of Armenia.
- Aksar Akayev elected president of Kyrgyzstan.
- Rakhman Nabiyev elected president of Tajikistan in an election marred by fraud.
- Ukraine votes for independence in a referendum. Leonid Kravchuk elected president.

- Islam Karimov elected president of Uzbekistan.
- Commonwealth of Independent States founded.
- President Gorbachev resigns from office on December 25. Soviet Union goes out of existence on December 31.

THE POST-SOVIET ERA

1992
Russia
- Yeltsin government begins economic reforms.
- Privatization program begins.
- Yeltsin dismisses Yegor Gaidar as prime minister and replaces him with Viktor Chernomyrdin.

Ukraine
- Russian ruble is replaced with a new Ukrainian currency.

Moldova
- Fighting breaks out in the Trans-Dniester region and lasts for several months until a cease-fire is arranged.

Lithuania
- Adopts new constitution.
- Parliament elects Algirdas Brazauskas president.

Estonia
- Lennart Meri elected president by parliament.
- Adopts a new constitution and issues a new currency, the *kroon*.

Georgia
- President Zviad Gamsakhurdia overthrown.
- Eduard Shevardnadze elected president. Parliament chosen in the same election is divided among thirty parties, none of which has a majority.

Azerbaijan
- President Ayaz Mutalibov is forced to resign because of defeats in Nagorno-Karabakh.
- Ali Elchibey becomes president.

Turkmenistan
- A new constitution adopted by referendum gives most power to the president and leaves the parliament weak. President Saparmurad Niyazov is reelected in an election in which he is the only candidate.

Tajikistan
- President Rakhman Nabiyev forced to resign because of the civil war that began in the spring.
- Emomali Rakhmonov emerges as president.

1993
Russia
- Signs START II nuclear arms treaty with the United States.
- Voters approve Yeltsin's economic policy in a referendum.
- Unsuccessful coup against Yeltsin led by leaders of parliament and Vice President Aleksandr Rutskoi.
- Elections to new parliament. LPD, led by Vladimir Zhirinovsky, leads in the proportional representation race. The Communist Party of the Russian Federation led by Gennadi Zyuganov also does well. Voters approve a new constitution that increases the power of the presidency.

Belarus
- Parliament dismisses President Stanislav Shushkevich from office.
- Parliament lifts ban on the Communist Party.

Latvia
- Elects new parliament.
- Parliament elects Guntis Ulmanis as president.

Lithuania
- Algirdas Brazauskas elected president in a popular election.
- Last Russian troops leave the country.

Estonia
- New citizenship law excludes most Russian residents.

Georgia
- Abkhazia falls to secessionists.
- Government bows to Russian pressure and joins the CIS.
- Zviad Gamsakhurdia dies under mysterious circumstances.

Azerbaijan
- Heydar Aliyev becomes president.
- Government bows to Russian pressure and rejoins the CIS.

Kazakhstan
- Adopts new constitution.
- Signs major oil development deal with the Chevron oil company.

- Forms Central Asian Economic Union with Uzbekistan and Kyrgyzstan.

1994
Russia
- President Yeltsin orders the Russian army into Chechnya to end the secessionist movement. Beginning of bitter and destructive fighting.
- Links economy with Belarus.

Ukraine
- Voters in the Crimean Peninsula elect secessionist Yury Meshkov as president.
- Voters elect new parliament. The newly reorganized Ukrainian Communist Party wins a plurality by taking one third of the seats.
- Leonid Kuchma elected president.

Belarus
- Adopts new constitution.
- Links economy with Russia.
- Aleksandr Lukashenko elected president.

Moldova
- Voters elect new parliament. Agrarian Party, which supports continued independence from Romania, wins the election.
- Signs agreement with Russia calling for Russian troops to leave Trans-Dniester region by 1997.
- Adopts new constitution.

Latvia
- New citizenship law excludes most Russian residents.
- Last Russian troops leave.

Estonia
- Last Russian troops leave.

Azerbaijan
- Signs major oil development deal with ten foreign oil companies, despite Russian objections.

Kazakhstan, Uzbekistan, Kyrgyzstan
- Three countries form an economic union.

Turkmenistan
- Niyazov "elected" president for life.

Tajikistan

- President Emomali Rakhmonov reelected and voters approve a new constitution. Opposition boycotts the election and referendum amid accusations of fraud.

1995
Russia

- Tightens military ties with Kazakhstan and economic and military ties with Belarus.
- Communist Party of the Russian Federation is the leading vote-getter in the parliamentary elections and wins a plurality in the new parliament.

Ukraine

- The Ukrainian parliament abolishes the constitution and the post of president of the Crimea.

Belarus

- Agrees with Russia to closer economic ties and to a common border defense.

Armenia

- Holds first post-Soviet election in which voters elect a parliament and adopt a new constitution.

Georgia

- Voters approve a new constitution. Eduard Shevardnadze survives an assassination attempt.

Kazakhstan

- Agrees to unify armed forces with Russia.
- Voters extend President Nursultan Nazarbayev's term until the year 2000.

Uzbekistan

- President Islam Karimov stages a referendum in which 99.6 percent of the voters agree to extend his term until the year 2000.

1996
Russia

- Andrei Kozyrev is forced out as foreign minister and replaced by Yevgeny Primakov.
- Agrees to "Council of Sovereign States" union with Belarus.

- Yeltsin appoints Aleksandr Lebed as his top-security adviser and fires Defense Minister Pavel Grachev.
- Yeltsin decisively defeats Gennadi Zyuganov in the runoff presidential election, 54 to 39 percent.
- Chechen rebels defeat Russian forces and retake Grozny.
- Lebed negotiates a cease-fire in Chechnya.
- Yeltsin fires Lebed from all his posts, replacing him as head of Russia's Security Council with Igor Rybkin.

Ukraine
- Adopts new constitution, the last post-Soviet country to do so, and introduces new currency.

Belarus
- Agrees to form a "Council of Sovereign Republics" with Russia.
- Amid charges of fraud, voters approve a referendum giving President Aleksandr Lukachenko sweeping new powers.

Moldova
- President Mercea Snegur is defeated in his reelection bid by Petru Lucinschi.

Tajikistan
- President Emomali Rakhmonov bows to rebel pressure and fires three corrupt officials. He appoints a new prime minister who promises economic reforms.

Russia, Belarus, Kazakhstan, Kyrgyzstan
- The four countries agree to strengthen their ties with each other, especially their economic relationships.

1997
Russia
- Signs peace treaty with Chechnya.
- Signs the Charter of the Russia-Belarus Union.
- Signs the NATO-Russia Founding Act.

Belarus
- Signs the Charter of the Russia-Belarus Union.

ENCYCLOPEDIA

INTRODUCTION

This encyclopedia section contains a variety of listings. It includes a biography of the current (1997) president of every post-Soviet state and a description of each of their capital cities. It also includes entries on important cities, rivers, lakes, and regions; significant ethnic groups; public figures in a variety of fields; and entries on a number of significant subjects, ranging from the problem of alcoholism to the lasting impact of the Chernobyl atomic accident. You can use this encyclopedia to supplement what you have learned from the essays in this book or as an independent source of information on the fifteen countries that have replaced the former Soviet Union.

Abuladze, Tengiz (1924–)
Prominent Georgian film director. Abuladze is best known for his 1986 film *Repentance*, which denounced Stalinism and totalitarianism in general.

Adamovich, Ales M. (1924–)

Belarusian writer and political figure. In 1966, Professor Adamovich was fired from Moscow State University for refusing to denounce two dissident writers, Andrei Siniavsky and Yuri Daniel. Since 1986, he has spoken out for Belarus as it struggles to recover from the Chernobyl disaster.

Aitmatov, Chingiz (1928–)

Kyrgyz writer. During the Soviet era, Aitmatov established his reputation as a serious writer while maintaining the approval of the Soviet establishment. Several of his important Soviet-era works, such as *The White Steamship* (1970), are a defense of rural life and traditional values against intrusion and destruction by the modern world. Aitmatov became a leading environmentalist and supporter of Gorbachev and perestroika. His 1986 novel *The Executioner's Block* exposed corruption in Central Asia.

Akayev, Aksar (1944–)

President of the Kyrgyz Republic. Akayev is a physicist and author of more than eighty scientific publications on fundamental physics. He served as vice president and then, from 1989 to 1990, as president of the Kyrgyz Academy of Sciences. He quit the Communist Party in August 1991. Akayev was elected president of his country in 1990 by the local Supreme Soviet. He was reelected to a second term in December 1995.

Akhmadulina, Bella (1937–)

Russia's most revered woman poet. Akhmadulina is descended from Italians on her mother's side and Tatars on her father's. Her poetry is admired for its extraordinary sense of language and form. With Yevgeny Yevtushenko, Andrei Voznesensky, and Vasily Aksyonov, she was a leader of the short-lived cultural revival that followed Khrushchev's denunciation of Stalin in the 1950s. In the  1970s the small and fragile Akhmadulina spoke up against repression of artists and intellectuals and called for the publication of Joseph Brodsky's poems. Many of her poems recall the memory of poets such as Osip Mandelstam and Marina Tsvetayeva, who suffered so terribly under Stalin, and Aleksandr Pushkin, Russia's greatest and most loved poet.

Aksyonov, Vasily P. (1932–)

One of several leading writers forced into exile during the Soviet era. Aksyonov is the son of Evgenia Ginzburg, whose unforgettable memoirs, *Journey Into the Whirlwind*, chronicled her eighteen years in Stalin's labor camps. Aksyonov was a leader in the cultural revival during the Khrushchev era. In 1979 he joined with more than twenty writers and poets to produce a collection called *Metropol*, which was published illegally, without approval of the Soviet censors. After his exile, Aksyonov's works were not published in the Soviet Union until the Gorbachev era. One book, *The Isle of Crimea*, then became a best-seller in his native land.

Alcoholism

One of Russia's (and Ukraine's and Belarus's) worst social problems, responsible for tens of thousands of deaths every year. Alcoholism has long been a Russian problem; travelers from Europe as far back as the sixteenth century commented on Russian drunkenness. The problem grew worse during the late Soviet period, when per person consumption of alcoholic beverages doubled. Mikhail Gorbachev's anti-alcohol campaign, one of his first steps after coming to power, ended in failure. When Boris Yeltsin ended price controls on most products in January 1992, one of the items not included was vodka, a sad commentary on what millions of Russians consider essential to their lives.

Aleksei II (Aleksei M. Ridiger) (1928–)
Patriarch of the Russian Orthodox Church. Elected in 1990, Aleksei's considerable influence on Russian life is symbolic of the revival of the Russian Orthodox Church.

Aliyev, Heydar A. (1923–)

President of Azerbaijan. Aliyev was born in the province of Nakhichevan, which today is cut off from the rest of Azerbaijan by a strip of Armenian territory. He became head of the local branch of the KGB in 1967 and over the next two years impressed his bosses in Moscow with his anticorruption drive. He also struck hard against Azerbaijani nationalists and pushed Russification policies, hardly suitable credentials for the future president of an independent Azerbaijan. Aliyev reached the Politburo, the highest Communist Party political body, in 1976. By the 1980s he was one of the dozen most powerful men in the Soviet Union, and one of the very few non-Slavs among its top leaders. He was demoted and pushed into retirement by Gorbachev in 1987. In 1990, he began his comeback by winning election to the local

parliament in Nakhichevan. The next year he resigned from the Communist Party, while continuing to build his power base in Nakhichevan, ultimately setting the stage for his return to power as his country's leader in 1992.

Almaty (Soviet era: Alma Ata)
The capital of Kazakhstan and also its largest city (population about 1.15 million). Its name means "City of Apples" in Kazakh. The city was the scene of the first large-scale ethnic riots during the Gorbachev era, when Gorbachev fired the corrupt ethnic-Kazakh head of the local Communist Party. Founded as a garrison town in 1854, it was used as a place to send political exiles, among them Leon Trotsky. On December 21, 1991, it was the site of the summit meeting at which eleven Soviet republics jointly declared the founding of the Commonwealth of Independent States (CIS). Current plans call for moving the capital to Akmola, a more centrally located city of 300,000 in the northern part of the country. The move is planned for the year 2000.

Aral Sea
An inland salt sea of 24,630 square miles (63,800 square kilometers), once the fourth-largest inland body of water in the

world. Soviet irrigation projects dating from the 1960s turned it into an environmental disaster by diverting the waters that used to flow into the Aral Sea to huge new cotton fields in Uzbekistan and Kazakhstan. By the 1990s the Aral Sea had lost more than 60 percent of its former surface area and 40 percent of its volume. Ports from which fishing boats once sailed now stood from 10 to 40 miles (16 to 64 kilometers) from the shore. Salt and chemical pollutants carried by winds from its dried-up bed have polluted vast areas and damaged the health of the local people.

Ashkhabat (Soviet era: Ashkabad)
The capital and largest city (population: 400,000) in Turkmenistan. Founded in 1881 as a garrison town shortly after the great battle at Geok-Tepe (see "Turkmenistan"). Totally destroyed in a 1948 earthquake that killed more than 100,000 people. Many of the people still live in temporary housing. Ashkhabat has been planted with many shade trees to give its people shelter from one of the hottest climates of any city in the former Soviet Union. Today the city has a gleaming new business and hotel center called Berzengi. It was built by order of President Saparmurad Niyazov. He expected it to be filled by crowds of Western businessmen, but they have yet to arrive. Berzengi's twenty-two ultramodern luxury hotels stand in the baking desert sun, mostly empty.

Baikal
There is no lake in the world like Lake Baikal, the "Pearl of Siberia." Formed more than 25 million years ago, it is the oldest and deepest lake in the world. It is more than 1 mile (1.6 kilometers) deep and holds one fifth of the world's freshwater supply, as much as all of North America's Great Lakes combined.

Fed by more than 300 rivers, it is home to more than 1,200 plant and animal species found nowhere else in the world.

The clarity and purity of Baikal's waters are legendary, and native peoples of the region have long been drawn to its shores to worship. But Baikal has been threatened with pollution since the 1960s, when the Soviet regime built the gigantic Baikalsk Cellulose-Paper Plant on its southern shore. Baikal immediately became a rallying cry for Russians concerned for their country's environment. But despite decades of efforts, the huge plant still pours 8.8 million cubic feet (250,000 cubic meters) of wastewater a day into the lake. This is particularly dangerous, because Baikal's "recycling period," the period of time over which its water is replaced, is 380 years, compared with only 10 years for the Great Lakes.

Baku
Oil center and capital of Azerbaijan. Where Baku stands today there has been a settlement for more than 2,500 years. A thousand years ago oil was scooped from hand-dug wells near the city. When foreign companies brought the modern oil industry to Baku in the 1880s, they turned the sleepy settlement into a boom town of opulent mansions but also caused severe pollution. Offshore drilling began in 1935 and soon crowded Baku's seascape with oil platforms. Baku and its oil became a prime Nazi target in World War II; their drive toward the vital region was stopped at Stalingrad (now Volgograd), in one of the decisive battles of the war. High walls

dating from the twelfth through the sixteenth century surround the old fortress town with its Islamic/Middle Eastern/Central Asian mosques and palaces. Many stone mansions recall the boom times before the revolution. The rest of Baku dates from the Soviet era.

Bishkek (Soviet era: Frunze)

Capital and largest city in Kyrgyzstan (population: about 600,000). Bishkek, like many Central Asian cities, began as a settlement along the ancient Silk Road that linked China with the Middle East and Europe. In 1825 the Khan of Kokand, one of the Central Asian states conquered by Russia in the mid-nineteenth century, built a fort near the settlement. The conquering Russians later turned it into a garrison town. During the Soviet era, the town was renamed for Mikhail Frunze, a Bolshevik military leader who was born there and, ironically, commanded Soviet forces that crushed Central Asian resistance to Soviet rule in the 1920s.

Brazauskas, Algirdas M. (1932–)

President of Lithuania. Educated as a civil engineer, Brazauskas rose through the ranks of the local Lithuanian Communist Party while working on issues involving construction, industry, and the economy. By the 1980s he had a reputation as a reformer and became the head of the local party organization in 1988. Like Gorbachev when he was head of the Communist Party in his native Stavropol, and unlike the traditional Communist Party leaders, Brazauskas made a point of walking in public without guards. His outgoing personality and booming voice fed his image as a populist. After losing out to Vytautas Landsbergis in the contest for Lithuania's presidency in 1990, Brazauskas was elected acting president by parliament in November 1992, and president in February 1993.

Brodsky, Joseph (1940–1996)

One of Russia's outstanding and outspoken twentieth-century poets. Born in Leningrad, Brodsky had his first collision with Soviet authorities when he was denied admission to the country's submarine academy because he was Jewish. He was fiercely independent and unafraid to write and publish poems that did not meet with the approval of Soviet authorities. Because he also associated with others unwilling to restrict what they said or wrote, Brodsky was arrested in 1964 and spent a year in prison. Only a few of his poems were published in his homeland before he was forced into exile in 1972. Brodsky settled in the United States, where he wrote poems and essays in both Russian and English that won him the Nobel Prize for literature in 1987. In 1990, he was the first foreign-born person appointed America's poet laureate. His death in 1996 from a heart attack caused great mourning among poetry lovers throughout the world.

Bukhara

An ancient trading city on Central Asia's Silk Road, Bukhara has gone through many ups-and-downs in its long history. As the capital of a large empire in the ninth and tenth centuries, Bukhara was Central Asia's Islamic cultural and religious center. Many of its Islamic-style architectural monuments date from the sixteenth century, when it once again was the capital of a Central Asian empire. Russia conquered the Khanate of Bukhara in the mid-nineteenth century. Despite its venerable past, Bukhara today is only Uzbekistan's fifth-largest city (population: about 230,000).

Burbulis, Gennadi E. (1945–)

One of Boris Yeltsin's top advisers and first deputy prime minister during 1991–1992. Burbulis was one of the men who worked intensively to draw up the document signed in Minsk in December 1991 that declared the end of the Soviet Union and the formation of the Commonwealth of Independent States. As first deputy prime minister, Burbulis was one of the architects of Yeltsin's economic reform program. Yeltsin was forced by conservative pressure to drop Burbulis from the government in April 1992, although he stayed on as an adviser.

Cathedral of the Holy Mother of Kazan
One of Moscow's most important Orthodox monuments, built in the seventeenth century and demolished on Stalin's orders in 1936 as part of his campaign to eliminate religious landmarks. For years the site remained a vacant lot; later it housed a public toilet. Plans to rebuild the church were approved by Moscow officials in 1990, and the church was reopened, with President Yeltsin in attendance, in November 1993. At the reconsecration, a priest commented, "The Kazan Cathedral is the monument to Russia's finding its full independence once and for all."[1]

Cathedral of the Holy Mother of Kazan

Chechnya

Secessionist Muslim republic of the Russian Federation in the North Caucasus region. The man who led Chechnya into attempted secession was Djohar Dudaev, its president until he was killed in April 1996. Boris Yeltsin's decision in December 1994 to send the Russian Army into Chechnya to crush the local independence movement led to tens of thousands of deaths and a military occupation of the republic in the face of an unending guerrilla war. It undermined Yeltsin's standing at home and discredited both the Russian government and its army abroad. In mid-August the Chechens dealt the Russians a decisive defeat when they retook Grozny, the republic's capital. A cease-fire agreement, the Khasavyurt accords, provided for the gradual withdrawal of Russian troops and a five-year transition period before the people of the republic decide its final status. However, it was clear that Russia's leaders remained intent on holding on to Chechnya, and Chechen leaders were intent on independence. In January 1997, Chechnya changed the name of its capital from Grozny to Djohar-gala, in honor of Djohar Dudaev. A few days later Chechen voters elected Aslan Maskhadov their new president. He was the overall commander of their military forces in the war with Russia. In May, calling itself the Republic of Ichkeria, Chechnya signed a peace treaty with Russia.

Chernobyl

The nuclear power plant in Ukraine where a reactor exploded and created the world's greatest nuclear disaster on April 26, 1986. According to the World Health Organization, the radiation released was about 200 times the combined radiation from the atomic bombs the United States dropped on Hiroshima and Nagasaki during World War II. Prevailing winds deposited most of the deadly radiation in northwestern Ukraine and southern and eastern Belarus, although about half of Europe received at least some radiation from the blast. While the plant was actually in Ukraine, it was Belarus that suffered the most damage. A total of about 54,000 square miles (140,000 square kilometers) in Ukraine, Belarus, and Russia were heavily contaminated.

The Chernobyl disaster occurred in large part because of flaws in the design of the plant—which is similar to fifteen plants still operating elsewhere in the former Soviet Union and in Eastern Europe—and because of carelessness and incompetence on the part of managers at the plant itself. Because there were no plans for evacuation in the event of a crisis, and because Soviet authorities tried to cover up the disaster, 49,000 people living in the town of Pripiat only a few miles from the plant were not evacuated for thirty-six hours. A week later, an additional 50,000 or more people who lived within an 18-mile (29-kilometer) radius of the plant (the "Exclusion Zone") were evacuated. Over the next four years, 100,000 more people had to move. In the desperate attempts to stop the fires, and during the long cleanup that followed, an estimated 800,000 workers were exposed to radiation. About 5 million people living in the region around Chernobyl in Belarus, Ukraine, and Russia also were exposed to varying radiation levels.

A Ukrainian government report in 1990 said that more than a million people, including 250,000 children, were living in areas where radiation was dangerously high. Some researchers estimate that 5,000 people already have died from diseases caused by radioactive fallout from the explosion. The World Health Organization reported in 1996 that the rate of thyroid cancer in children in the most exposed region was 100 times the normal rate. Large areas, including some of the most fertile areas of Belarus, cannot be farmed because of contaminated soil. Villages, farms, and towns remain deserted, unsafe for human habitation. In 1996, Belarus was spending 15 percent of its gross national product caring for people dislocated or made ill by the Chernobyl disaster. Another report noted genetic damage in children born in the decade since the explosion.

Despite the costs and dangers, ten years after the disaster the other three reactors at Chernobyl were still operating. The Ukrainian government had promised to close the plant eight times, and then reversed itself every time, mainly because the Chernobyl plant produced electricity and provided thousands of jobs that Ukraine's government believed the country could not afford to lose.

Chernomyrdin, Viktor S. (1938–)

Prime Minister of the Russian Federation. Chernomyrdin rose up through the ranks of the Communist Party while working in industrial management, eventually becoming head of the Soviet natural-gas monopoly. He did not leave the Communist Party until 1991. In 1988, during the Gorbachev

era, Chernomyrdin played a major role in turning the ministry into a state-owned company called Gazprom. When the company was privatized under Yeltsin (the government still owns 40 percent), Chernomyrdin, like many other Communist Party bosses in various industries, used his connections to make himself a millionaire. In December 1992, in a compromise with conservative critics of his economic policies, President Yeltsin appointed Chernomyrdin to be Russia's prime minister. Despite his own criticism of Yeltsin's radical economic reforms, Chernomyrdin continued to move Russia toward a market economy, demonstrating sound judgment and winning respect both in Russia and abroad. He moved out of Yeltsin's shadow and won considerable admiration in 1995 when, on live television, he negotiated the end of the hostage crisis in the town of Budyonnovsk, where Chechen gunmen had seized more than 1,000 hostages. Chernomyrdin's star dimmed temporarily when his newly founded moderate Our Home Is Russia political party did poorly in the December 1995 parliamentary elections.

However, he worked hard in Yeltsin's successful reelection campaign and was reappointed prime minister immediately after the election. In the wake of the 1996 presidential election, Chernomyrdin's impressive performance as prime minister and the support he provided Yeltsin left him as the second most powerful man in Russia.

Chisinau (Soviet era: Kishinev)

Capital of Moldova. Virtually rebuilt after suffering terrible destruction during World War II, Chisinau is a modern city filled with parks and trees. It was a small town until Russia annexed the region it called Bessarabia in the early nineteenth century and made Chisinau into a regional capital. A small area of narrow winding streets near the shore of the Bik River is all that remains of the old part of the city.

Chornovil, Viacheslav (1938–)
Leader of Rukh, the nationalist movement that played a major role in moving Ukraine toward independence during the Gorbachev era and that remains a major force in Ukrainian politics today. Chornovil spent ten years in prison during the Soviet era for his nationalist activities. A staunch anti-Communist, he finished second to Leonid Kravchuk in Ukraine's first presidential elections in 1991. Under his leadership, Rukh has followed a moderate course. It supports free-market reforms, the legal equality of all citizens, and Ukraine's orientation toward the West. In contrast to more extreme Ukrainian nationalist leaders, Chornovil also has supported his country's developing relations with Russia.

Chubais Anatoly B. (1955–)
First Russian Deputy Prime Minister. One of the youthful free-market reformers associated with Yegor Gaider, Chubais's first government post was as head of the department that implemented Boris Yeltsin's privatization program beginning in 1992. Despite being blamed by opponents of economic reform and the public in general for the problems associated with privatization, Chubais remained in the cabinet until January 1996, when Yeltsin finally forced him out in the wake of the 1995 parliamentary elections. Chubais nonetheless supported Yeltsin in the 1996 presidential elections, mainly to prevent a Communist victory. After playing a key role in Yeltsin's successful reelection cam-

paign, Chubais was appointed the president's chief of staff. In March 1997, Chubais became one of Russia's most powerful political figures when Yeltsin appointed him first deputy prime minister.

Commonwealth of Independent States (CIS)

The organization that replaced the Soviet Union. Its original membership of eleven (see Chapter I) at first dropped to ten when Azerbaijan left the organization. However, during 1993 both Azerbaijan and Georgia, desperate for Russian support against secessionist movements (see Chapter V), bowed to Russian pressure and became CIS members. Although as of 1996 its members had signed a total of 300 agreements, the CIS remained a vaguely defined organization whose main function seemed to be its use by Russia to maintain influence.

Cossacks

Fiercely independent peasant warriors and adventurers of the Eurasian steppe. The origin of the name "Cossack" tells a great deal about them; it comes from a Turkish word meaning "free man." The Cossacks were runaway serfs who settled on the frontiers of the Russian Empire. They mixed with local inhabitants and were famous as horsemen and fighters. Depending on where they settled, different Cossack groups spoke Russian or Ukrainian, but they clung to their Cossack identity. Ultimately the Cossacks were unable to maintain their independence in the face of the expanding Russian Empire. However, Cossack chieftains Stenka Razin (in 1670–1671) and Emelian Pugachev (1773–1775) led the two greatest peasant rebellions in Russian history. Later, Cossacks served as elite troops for the tsars. They helped to expand the empire and crush opposition to the tsars' autocratic rule, often with great brutality. Since the fall of the Soviet Union, some Cossacks have been reviving their old traditions. While there were about 4 million Cossacks in the Russian Empire, perhaps a million are taking part in the current revival. Still, they remain an integral and colorful, as well as controversial, part of both Russian and Ukrainian history.

Crimean Peninsula

Russia took the Crimean Peninsula in 1783 from the declining Ottoman Empire during the reign of Catherine the Great, who called the picturesque peninsula the finest pearl in her crown. And it is a pearl, especially its southeastern coast, which, sheltered from chilling northern winds by the 90-mile (145-kilometer)-long Crimean Mountains, enjoys a mild Mediterranean climate with 250 sunny days per year. Under the tsars and Soviets alike, privileged Russians have flocked to the Crimea for vacations. Mikhail Gorbachev was vacationing in the Crimea when the August coup against him took place.

The main playground of the Crimea is Yalta, whose hills are dotted with many pre-Revolutionary palaces and mansions. Among them is Tsar Nicholas II's Marble Palace, site of the Yalta Conference of 1945. That historic meeting during the waning days of World War II between Franklin Roosevelt, Winston Churchill, and Joseph Stalin set the stage for the Cold War.

The Marble Palace in the Crimea

Today's problems involving the Crimea stem from Nikita Khrushchev's 1954 decision—meaningless at the time, given the existence of the Soviet Union—to transfer the Crimea from Russian jurisdiction to the Ukraine. He called the transfer a "gift" in "honor" of 300 years of Russian-Ukrainian "unity." When that "unity," really Russian control, ended in December 1991, the Crimea, whose population is 70 percent Russian, suddenly belonged to an independent Ukraine, against the wishes of most of its inhabitants. Their desire to secede and rejoin Russia has been a constant source of tension between Russia and Ukraine.

One part of the Crimea that evokes a particularly emotional response from Russians is the port city of Sevastopol. It was the site of heroic Russian resistance to British, French, and Turkish forces in the Crimean War, falling only after a devastating 349-day siege in 1854–1855. One of the Russian defenders at Sevastopol was a young officer named Leo Tolstoy. When not directing artillery barrages, he sat in a bombproof bunker 200 yards (180 meters) from enemy lines and chronicled the battle in *Sevastopol Tales*, the work that first gave him a national reputation. In World War II, Sevastopol again held out against overwhelming odds during the German siege of 1942, this time falling after 250 days.

Dnieper River (Ukrainian: Dnipro)
National river of Ukraine. The Dnieper River, upon whose banks the city of Kiev is built, also is the waterway that flows through the histories of all three East Slavic peoples. It rises near Moscow, then flows through Belarus before entering Ukraine on its long journey to the Black Sea. The Dnieper is the third-longest river in Europe (1,430 miles, or 2,300 kilometers), trailing only the Volga and the Danube.

The Dnieper was part of the famous trade route linking Scandinavia and the Byzantine Empire in pre-Kievian and Kievian times. Its banks and surrounding countryside were the core of Kievian Russia. In the sixteenth century, Cossacks built a power center along its banks. These Zaporozhe Cossacks were Ukrainian-speaking and took a leading role in the great seventeenth-century Ukrainian revolt against Poland. The famous rapids near which the Cossacks lived were submerged by a Soviet hydroelectric station built between 1927 and 1932.

Don River

Like the Volga, the Don flows through much of the Russian heartland. It rises south of Moscow and flows into the Sea of Azov. In 1380 one of the decisive battles of Russia's history took place on a field near the Don when Prince Dmitri of Moscow defeated the Tatars of the Golden Horde. Dmitri's victory, while it did not break the Tatar hold on Russia, shattered the Tatars' image of invincibility. Half of both armies were killed or wounded in the brutal battle; it took the Russians a week to bury their dead. The battle became a symbol of Russia's national revival; Dmitri became known as Dmitri Donskoi, or Dmitri of the Don. In later centuries Cossacks colonized the lower Don and, as the Don Cossacks, made it their most important center.

Donbass (also called Donets Basin)

The huge and enormously important mining and industrial region in the eastern part of Ukraine. The Donbass was the most important coal-producing and iron-manufacturing region of the Russian Empire, and its industrial sector was developed further under the Soviet regime. In July 1989, Donbass coal miners staged the first major strike in the Soviet Union in almost three decades. This part of eastern Ukraine has a large Russian population. In 1993, when Donbass coal miners went on strike over price increases, their demands included autonomy for their region. There is some support among local Russians for secession from Ukraine and reunification with Russia.

Dudaev, Djohar M. (1944–1996) President of Chechnya, 1991–1996. A former Soviet air force officer, Dudaev seized power in Chechnya in 1991 and confirmed his status as president in a rigged election. In his reckless determination to break away from Russia, Dudaev led his people into a devastating war when his refusal to compromise drove Boris Yeltsin to send the Russian army to crush Chechnya's secession movement. Despite the appalling loss of life and having his forces driven from most of Chechnya, Dudaev continued to fight. He was killed in April 1996 when the Russians used advanced electronic tracking equipment to home in on Dudaev while he was speaking on a satellite phone. Meanwhile, Chechnya lay in ruins and the killing continued until Chechen forces retook Grozny (now named Djohar-gala, in Dudaev's honor) and a cease-fire was negotiated in August.

Dushanbe

Capital and largest city in Tajikistan (population: about 600,000). For more than thirty years the city was called Stalinabad; its name was changed back to Dushanbe in 1961 during Khrushchev's anti-Stalinist campaign. Dushanbe grew into a major city after the Soviet regime built a railroad into the region. Because of the threat of earthquakes, buildings in the city are either only a few floors high or specially engineered to ensure structural integrity.

Dyachenko, Tatiana, (1959–)

Daughter of Boris Yeltsin and considered by many to be his closest adviser. Dubbed "The Kremlin Princess" by the Russian press, Dyachenko emerged as her father's closest adviser. After Yeltsin was reelected president, she persuaded him to appoint Anatoly Chubais as his chief of staff. The wife of an engineer/businessman and the mother of two sons, Dyachenko also played a crucial role in Yeltsin's decision to fire Aleksandr Korzhakov.

Elbrus

Highest mountain in Europe. Located in Russia's North Caucasus region, Mt. Elbrus is topped by a volcanic cone with two peaks, the higher western peak reaching 18,510 feet (5,642 meters) above sea level. Its name, which comes from Persian, means "two heads."

Extremist Nationalism: Russian and Ukrainian

The collapse of communism and the Soviet Union has resulted in the revival of extremist nationalist sentiment in Russia. There are at least eighty ultranationalist groups of varying influence in the country. These groups are particularly bitter about Russia's diminished place in the world. They also feed on Russia's economic hardship. They tend to be anti-Western and hostile to non-Russians, especially Jews. Anti-Semitism, in fact, is one of their common and most frequently expressed themes.

Vladimir Zhirinovsky is only the best known of many extreme nationalist Russian political figures. One group that got its start even before Zhirinovsky and his Liberal Democratic Party is Pamiat (Memory), which dates from the mid-1980s. It was founded by a convicted murderer named Dmitri Vasiliev. Another highly influential figure in the ultranationalist camp is Alexander Prokhanov, editor of the newspaper *Zavtra* (Tomorrow). Prokhanov helped forge an alliance between nationalist groups and the Communist Party of the Russian Federation led by Gennadi Zyuganov that has the potential to take control of Russian political life.

Ukraine also has a variety of extremist nationalist organizations. The most influential is the UNA-UNSO (Ukrainian National Assembly–Ukrainian National Self Defense). The organization opposes democracy and stresses that it will rely heavily on the army and the secret police if it comes to power. It is deeply hostile to Russia and seeks Russia's complete disintegration and its replacement by a new Slavic empire led by what it calls "Great Ukraine." The UNA-UNSO has its own paramilitary force of between 3,000 and 4,000 members.

Federal Security Service (FSB in Russian letters)

The successor to the notorious Soviet KGB operating inside Russia. The FSB controls the most important internal security arms of the former KGB. (Foreign intelligence is handled by the Foreign Intelligence Service—SVR in Russian letters—the other main successor to the KGB.) When Boris Yeltsin took power in late December 1991 he promised to completely reform the KGB. However, his reform program soon lapsed, as he began using the security forces as a power base. In February 1995, as part of Yeltsin's war on crime, the FSB was given extensive new powers to spy on Russian citizens. One newspaper complained that these powers "allow the Lubyanka (a reference to the KGB's address) to cover the entire country with secret agents again."[2] In June 1996, after Yeltsin fired three of his top hard-line conservative advisers, he appointed Nikolai Kovalev to head the FSB.

Fergana Valley

More than 2,000 years ago, the Chinese came to the Fergana Valley, a strip of land with fertile oases that passes through Kyrgyzstan, Tajikistan, and Uzbekistan, to buy its famous "dragonhorses." During the Soviet era, the 186-mile (300-kilometer) - long valley was used to grow cotton and fruit and to raise silkworms. Today poverty and weak government controls have turned the Fergana Valley into a center for the opium trade. Drug trafficking has become an enormous business throughout Central Asia since the fall of the Soviet Union. One of its main centers is Osh, a city in Kyrgyzstan's part of the Fergana Valley.

Gaidar, Yegor T. (1956–)

Economist and former deputy prime minister for economic affairs and acting prime minister under Boris Yeltsin. Gaidar, born in Moscow, was the architect of Yeltsin's "shock therapy" economic reform program. Yeltsin appointed him acting prime minister in April 1992, but was forced by conservative pressure to replace him with Viktor Chernomyrdin in December of that year. Gaidar returned to the Yeltsin cabinet in September 1993 as one of its four deputy prime ministers and the economic minister, but resigned his posts in January 1994 over policy differences with the president. His political party, Russia's Choice (since 1994, Russia's Democratic Choice), did well in the 1993 parliamentary elections but very poorly in the 1995 elections.

Germans

Most of the Germans in the former Soviet Union are descendants of colonists that Empress Catherine the Great, herself a German, invited to Russia in the 1770s. Most settled and established farms along the Volga River. They remained there until they were deported to Central Asia and Siberia during World War II. They were kept in remote camps until 1955, when they were allowed to resettle in parts of the Urals region, in Kazakhstan, and western Siberia.

Official estimates place the number of ethnic Germans in the former Soviet Union at about 2 million. However, if those who have hidden their German identity and those who are partially German are included, the actual number may reach 5 million. In the mid-1970s the Soviet regime permitted a small but continuous emigration to West Germany. The level of emigration increased significantly during the Gorbachev era and jumped again after the collapse of the Soviet Union. The future of the Germans in the former Soviet Union now is very cloudy. It is likely that about 90 percent of them would like to emigrate to Germany. But Germany currently is dealing with the expensive task of rebuilding the former East Germany, and is therefore not enthusiastic about a large influx of people who will need considerable government help for the foreseeable future. Meanwhile, the ethnic Germans feel insecure and unwelcome where they live, whether in Kazakhstan, Russia, or any other post-Soviet state. By 1996, about two thirds of the Germans living in Kazakhstan as of 1990 had emigrated to Germany. As one German diplomat who was sent to Kazakhstan to help ethnic Germans there build a better future put it, "They don't want to create a better future here. They want to pack."[3]

Gorbachev, Mikhail S. (1931–)

Leader of the Soviet Union from 1985 to 1991. Gorbachev's policies of perestroika and glasnost were intended to reform the Soviet Union by overhauling its economy and making it more democratic. Instead, they set in motion forces that proved uncontrollable and led to its disintegration. Yet while Gorbachev ultimately failed to achieve his goals, his policies led to the end of the Cold War, for which he is highly respected in the West. He is, however, very unpopular in Russia, blamed for causing the collapse of the Soviet Union and the hard times that Russia has undergone since the late 1980s. Out of office since 1991, he has headed a think tank called the International Foundation for Social, Economic, and Political Research, better known as the Gorbachev Foundation. He became a vocal critic of many of Boris Yeltsin's policies, and in 1996 ran against him for president, receiving less than 1 percent of the vote. When asked why he was running despite obviously having little support, Gorbachev answered: "I set the course that has given the people the right to make this choice. Who more than I has a right to run?"[4]

Grachev, Pavel S. (1948–)

Russian defense minister, 1992–1996. Grachev earned Boris Yeltsin's gratitude and respect when, in August 1991, as commander of the Soviet Union's airborne troops, he refused to back the coup against Mikhail Gorbachev. Grachev's refusal to bring an elite airborne division to Moscow to storm Yeltsin's headquarters at the White House was one of the crucial acts that thwarted the anti-Gorbachev plotters. General Grachev came to Yeltsin's defense at a critical time again in October 1993,

when he ordered his troops to attack the White House, at that time the barricaded headquarters of Yeltsin's opponents in parliament. However, Grachev was accused of corruption and was widely disliked. His reputation was further hurt by his support of the war in Chechnya, where Russia's army performed poorly after he boasted his paratroopers could easily handle the Chechens. Nonetheless, despite pressure from many sources, President Yeltsin stuck by Grachev. In June 1996, when Yeltsin brought Aleksandr Lebed, a bitter critic of Grachev, into his government to strengthen his position in the upcoming runoff presidential election, he finally had to fire his defense minister.

Jews

No minority in the former Soviet Union suffered from persecution and discrimination as severely as the Jews. Millions of Jews emigrated in the late nineteenth and early twentieth centuries to escape tsarist persecution, many of them coming to the United States. While anti-Semitism officially was illegal during the Soviet era, Jews still faced discrimination. After the Germans invaded the Soviet Union in 1941, they murdered more than 1.5 million Soviet Jews. Anti-Jewish policies in the USSR reached their peak after the Holocaust, when Stalin conducted a vicious anti-Semitic campaign from 1948 until his death in 1953. After enduring further discrimination under Khrushchev and Brezhnev, Soviet Jews organized and demanded the right to emigrate to Israel. Largely because of pressure from the United States, several hundred thousand Jews were allowed to leave the Soviet Union in the 1970s. Most went to Israel.

Since the fall of the Soviet Union, emigration to Israel has increased. Jews who choose to remain in the post-Soviet states face a contradictory situation. Like other groups, Jews now have religious freedom and there has been a revival of organized Jewish life. At the same time, Jews face increasing anti-Semitism, especially in Ukraine and Russia, as people enduring hard times look for a scapegoat. The leading anti-Semitic politician, but hardly the only one, in the former Soviet Union is Vladimir Zhirinovsky. Many organizations and publications in both Russia and Ukraine are openly anti-Semitic.

The number of Jews in the former Soviet Union is difficult to estimate because many Jews, especially half-Jews, in the past chose to hide their Jewish identity. A reasonable guess is that 1.6 million Jews remain in Russia, perhaps 500,000 in Ukraine, and as many as 2.5 million in the former Soviet Union as a whole.

Kadannikov, Vladimir V. (1941–)

Russia's deputy prime minister in charge of the economy. Kadannikov replaced Anatoly Chubais, the last strong advocate of free-market reforms in Boris Yeltsin's cabinet, in January 1996. An engineer by training, he rose through the ranks during the Soviet era to head the giant Avtovaz automobile plant—Russia's largest, with more than 100,000 employees. That plant, like the Soviet auto industry itself, is notorious for its inefficiency. Kadannikov is an advocate of protective tariffs to avoid what he calls the "death of all national industry."[5] One leading Western economist, expressing his concern over the appointment of Kadannikov and what it might mean for reform in Russia, commented: "This is the first time they [the Russians] have had a chief economist who is not an economist."[6]

Kaliningrad

Russian city and surrounding territory, wedged between Lithuania, Poland, and the Baltic Sea. The city of Kaliningrad is the old German city of Königsberg, founded by German knights in the mid-thirteenth century. It was part of the German territory of East Prussia that was taken from Germany after World War II and divided between Poland and Russia. Russia took the 23,000-square-mile (59,570-square-kilometer) portion that includes Kaliningrad. The city itself was totally destroyed during World War II and its German population expelled by the Soviet army. Königsberg's name was changed to Kaliningrad, after a Soviet political figure, and it was resettled almost entirely with ethnic Russians. However, with the collapse of the Soviet Union, the Kaliningrad enclave, with its population of about 900,000, was cut off from the rest of Russia by newly independent Lithuania. Its relationship with its neighbors is now in some ways uncertain—one observer referred to it as "The Nowhere City"—although Russia definitely is not going to give up the last prize in Europe that it holds from World War II.

Karimov, Islam A. (1938–)

President of Uzbekistan. Like most of the national leaders of Central Asia, Karimov, a former Communist Party official, rules his country as a dictator. "We live in a police state that would have made the old Bolsheviks proud," says former prime minister and vice president Shukrulla Mirsaidov, one of the few opposition figures who have not fled Uzbekistan.[7] Karimov's supporters counter that his rule has provided stability, and point to the instability elsewhere in Central Asia, especially in war-torn Tajikistan to the east and Afghanistan to the south, as far less desirable alternatives.

Kasparov, Gary (1963–)

World chess champion. Kasparov is of Armenian-Jewish descent. He won the Soviet chess championship at age eighteen and the world championship four years later. After 1985, Kasparov was identified with the reformist and democratic forces in the Soviet Union. Anatoly Karpov, the man Kasparov defeated for the title, was identified with the Soviet establishment. Their matches, including Kasparov's successful defense of his title, therefore took on a political overtone.

Kharkiv (Kharkov in Soviet Era)

Second-largest city in Ukraine (population: 1.6 million). Kharkiv was founded as a Cossack outpost in 1654. Although it is in the eastern part of Ukraine that is heavily Russian and only 25 miles (40 kilometers) from the Russian border, more than half of Kharkiv's population is Ukrainian. Kharkiv has had a university since 1805, and during the nineteenth century it became a Ukrainian cultural and intellectual center. It has been an industrial center since the 1870s.

Kharkiv was the capital of Soviet Ukraine from 1917 until 1934. The site of major battles during World War II, the city changed hands five times and was left in ruins. It was rebuilt after the war into a manufacturing center that produced major industrial machines such as tractors, turbines, and engines. Today it once again has an active cultural life.

Khasbulatov, Ruslan (1942–)

Speaker of the Russian Federation parliament, 1991–1993. An ethnic Chechen and a former economics professor, Khasbulatov was elected to the Gorbachev-era parliament, the Congress of People's Deputies, in 1990 from his native Chechnya. When Boris Yeltsin was elected Russia's president in June 1991, he backed Khasbulatov to succeed him as the parliament's chairman, or speaker. He remained an ally of Yeltsin through the August 1991 coup, but along with Alexander Rutskoi, Khasbulatov turned against Yeltsin over the issue of economic reform. With Rutskoi, he led the October coup against Yeltsin, was arrested when the coup failed, and was released with the other plotters of the August 1991 and October 1993 coups when the anti-Yeltsin parliament voted them amnesties. He did not play a visible role in the Chechen-Russian war in his homeland.

Kiev (Kyiv in Ukrainian)

Capital and largest city (population: 2.6 million) in Ukraine. Kiev is the "Mother of Russian cities" to all the East Slavs. First settled in the fifth century, Kiev officially celebrated its 1,500th anniversary in 1982. It became a major trading center in the eighth century because of its prime location on the Dnieper River, along the "water road" from the Baltic Sea to Constantinople. In the ninth century it became the capital of Kievian Russia and the most important city in the region.

By the eleventh century, Kiev was an impressive cultural and political center that compared favorably with major cities elsewhere in Europe. Among its hundreds of churches was majestic St. Sophia's Cathedral, which today is Kiev's oldest standing church. The cathedral also housed Kievian Russia's first school and library and served as the site for important political events such as coronations. About 2 miles (3 kilometers) away was the Monastery of the Caves, an entire complex of churches, monasteries, and underground chambers filled with mummified monks. Kiev's princes lived on a hill overlooking the Dnieper River. Along the river were the homes of merchants and craftsmen.

In 1240, Kiev suffered almost total destruction at the hands of invading Mongols. A visitor from Western Europe six years later found only 200 houses standing. Kiev's next period of rapid growth began in the late eighteenth century after Russia consolidated its hold on most of Ukraine. However, the tsarist government also encouraged Russian settlement in Kiev and pushed Russification policies. In the 1930s, Kiev grew as a result of Soviet industrialization policies. By 1939 its population was about 850,000. The city was taken in September 1941 by the invading Germans, who then turned a ravine called Babi Yar just outside the city into a killing field for tens of thousands of Jews. By the time the Soviets retook Kiev more than two years later, most of the city lay in ruins and about 80 percent of its people were homeless. Kiev grew very quickly in the decades after the war as a result of further Soviet industrialization and housing construction.

Because of wartime destruction, most of Kiev was rebuilt during the 1950s and 1960s. Today Kiev is a city of urban sprawl, modern avenues, and spacious squares. Despite Ukraine's economic troubles since independence, private businesses increasingly line its streets, including the mile-long Kreshchatik, Kiev's busy main boulevard.

Kiselev, Yvgeny A. (1956–)

Host of *Itogi* (Results), Russia's most important television weekly news show. Kiselev moved into broadcast journalism after working as an interpreter for the Soviet military in Afghanistan and as a language teacher at a KGB school. He has a deserved reputation for telling his listeners the truth and therefore is considered extremely influential. Kiselev probably is one of the most popular men in Russia.

Korzhakov, Aleksandr V. (1940–)

Former chief of security for Russia's President Yeltsin. In addition to his formal post as Yeltsin's security chief, which made him Yeltsin's chief bodyguard, Korzhakov was a trusted adviser and the president's closest friend. In 1985 the KGB assigned Korzhakov to protect Yeltsin after he was brought to Moscow by Mikhail Gorbachev. He stood beside Yeltsin in front of the White House during the August 1991 coup against Gorbachev. Korzhakov probably was the most important of the small group of advisers—which included former defense minister Pavel Grachev and former chief of staff Sergei Filatov—that Yeltsin increasingly relied on by 1993 as he turned away from reformers like Yegor Gaidar and Andrei Kozyrev. One Western diplomat expressed a commonly held view of Korzhakov in May

1996, "He's the scariest guy in the Russian government."[8] After the first round of the presidential elections in June 1996, amid rumors that Korzhakov was planning some kind of coup and intending to cancel the runoff elections, Yeltsin reluctantly dismissed his friend. However, Korzhakov remained well connected and a powerful political force.

Kovalev, Sergei A. (1930–)

Former head of Russia's Presidential Human Rights Commission and parliamentary Human Rights Commission. Kovalev is a biologist and former dissident who spent many years in Soviet prison camps. He was a close friend of the late Andrei Sakharov, the most prominent dissident of the Brezhnev era. Kovalev was attacked for his unyielding opposition to the Chechnya war; he stayed in the center of Grozny during the heaviest bombing of the city by Russian planes. In 1995, the same year he was nominated for the Nobel Peace Prize, Russia's parliament dismissed Kovalev from its human rights commission. He resigned from the Presidential Human Rights Commission in January 1996 in protest against what he considered Boris Yeltsin's increasingly authoritarian policies. Kovalev remains an important figure and symbol in Russia; he has been called Russia's most respected democrat.

Kozyrev, Andrei V. (1951–)

Reformist and pro-Western foreign minister of Russia from 1991 to January 1996. Kozyrev, who is fluent in both English and French, was the architect of Russia's pro-Western foreign

policy during Russia's first post-Soviet years. That policy, which included major steps in reducing nuclear arms, was strongly criticized by nationalist and Communist forces. He remained at his post even when Yeltsin, responding to the growing power of his critics, began taking a harder line toward the West in 1993. However, after heavy criticism from Yeltsin, Kozyrev finally resigned in January 1996. He remained in public life, however, having won a seat in parliament in the December 1995 elections.

Kravchuk, Leonid M. (1934–)

President of independent Ukraine until 1994. A loyal Communist who did not resign from the party until August 1991, Kravchuk nonetheless managed to adopt enough of a nationalist posture to be elected president in December 1991. While working to assure Ukraine's independence, Kravchuk also agreed to give up all of Ukraine's nuclear weapons. His failure to prevent economic hardship undermined his popularity, and he was soundly defeated in the July 1994 presidential race by Leonid Kuchma.

Kuchma, Leonid (1938–)

President of Ukraine, elected in July 1994. Educated as an engineer and a man with wide experience, Kuchma once headed the largest missile factory in the Soviet Union. He also served briefly as Ukraine's prime minister under President Kravchuk. Kuchma ran on a platform advocating economic reform and closer ties with Russia. He received overwhelming support from Ukraine's 11 million ethnic Russians, who are concentrated in the eastern part of the country. While promising to preserve Ukraine's independence, Kuchma also stressed his country;s need for closer economic ties with Russia.

Ladoga

The largest lake in Europe, located just northeast of St. Petersburg. Lake Ladoga played a major role in saving St. Petersburg after the invading German army surrounded the city in the fall of 1941. The only outlet to Soviet-controlled territory was across a corner of the lake. When Ladoga's waters froze that winter, a "Road of Life" was built across the ice to supply the city. The lake, which has an area of more than 7,000 square miles (18,130 square kilometers), holds the largest reserve of freshwater in Europe. But it has been heavily polluted and is near biological death. Efforts by environmentalists to fight pollution since the mid-1980s have met with little success. In 1990 a boat wreck was discovered at the lake's bottom, which had been leaking radioactivity for thirty years.

Landsbergis, Vytautas V. (1932–)

First president of independent Lithuania. He began his career as a musicologist and for many years was a professor at the Lithuanian Conservatory. In 1988 he became one of the founders of the Sajudis movement, was elected to the Soviet parliament (the Congress of People's Deputies) in 1989, and chosen as chairman of the Lithuanian parliament—which made him the country's president—in 1990. Landsbergis showed steely determination in standing up to Moscow in the various crises that accompanied his struggle to bring about Lithuanian independence. After independence, Lithuania's economic troubles undermined his popularity. After Sajudis was defeated in the 1992 parliamentary elections, Landsbergis was replaced as president by his long-time rival, Algirdas Brazauskas.

Lazarenko, Pavlo (1953–)
Prime minister of Ukraine. An agricultural specialist during the Soviet era, Lazarenko was appointed to the position of first deputy prime minister in 1995. He became his country's prime minister in May 1996.

Lebed, Aleksandr (1950–)
Head of Russia's Security Council briefly, from June to October in 1996 and during that period President Yeltsin's top military and security adviser. Lebed, a military hero, is a former general and former commander of the Soviet Fourteenth Army stationed in the Trans-Dniester region of Moldova. Lebed began his military career as a paratrooper and rose to become deputy commander of  Soviet airborne forces. It is believed that while he was in command the Fourteenth Army assisted ethnic Russian secessionist forces in Moldova. Enormously popular with his sol-

diers and widely respected in Russia, Lebed strongly criticized the war in Chechnya. His criticism of the government led to his forced resignation from the army in July 1995. Lebed's political beliefs are nationalist and authoritarian. He believed Russia was not ready for democracy and called for the restoration of Russia's Soviet-era borders. He also strongly criticized Yeltsin's economic reforms. Although the party he was closely associated with—the Congress of Russian Communities—did poorly in the 1995 elections, Lebed won a seat in parliament and emerged as a candidate for Russia's presidency.

In the first round of the presidential elections in June 1996, Lebed finished third with an impressive 15 percent of the vote. Within a few days Yeltsin appointed the former general to head Russia's National Security Council. Lebed's support was considered important in Yeltsin's ultimate victory in July over Communist candidate Gennadi Zyuganov. In the wake of the election, Lebed distanced himself from his previous support of Communist positions, observing that communism "hasn't worked anywhere." He also made no secret that he wanted to succeed Yeltsin as president. Yeltsin fired Lebed from all his posts in October 1996. Lebed lives modestly and recently gave up drinking, commenting that "There should be at least one man in Russia who is sober."[9]

Literature
Historian Bertram Wolfe once wrote that after the thirteenth century Russia was a "strangely silent land." He was referring to its failure to produce any great writers or poets over the next five hundred years. Russia "remained silent" as other European countries such as Italy, England, France, and Spain produced literary figures such as Dante, Shakespeare, Racine, and Cervantes. Wolfe added that when Russia, "suddenly full throated," finally found its voice in the nineteenth century, "it astonished the world."[10]

That astonishment began when Aleksandr Pushkin (1799–1837) burst on the scene with his plays, prose, and, most important, his poems. Pushkin, still revered as Russia's greatest poet, began the "golden age" of Russian literature. His poem "The Bronze Horseman" and *Eugene Onegin*, a novel written as a narrative poem, are among the classics of world literature. Pushkin's own early and tragic death—he was killed in a duel when he was thirty-seven—stands as a symbol of an enduring Russian experience: senseless violence that plagues the country from generation to generation. Pushkin was followed by Mikhail Lermontov (1814–1841) and Nikolai Gogol (1809–1852). Like Pushkin, Lermontov was outstanding as both poet and prose writer. Also like Pushkin, whose death he mourned in his poem "Death of a Poet," Lermontov was killed in a senseless duel. And like Pushkin and so many of Russia's great cultural figures, he suffered government oppression. "The Demon," Lermontov's greatest poem, was not published during his lifetime because of tsarist censorship.

Gogol was of Ukrainian birth but wrote in Russian. His novel *Dead Souls* and play *The Inspector General* are Russian classics.

The giants of the Russian novel are Fyodor Dostoyevsky (1821–1881) and Leo Tolstoy (1828–1910). They brought the golden age to its magnificent peak. Each man wrote several novels that rank with the greatest ever written. As a young man, Dostoyevsky was almost hanged for his part in a plot against the tsar. His novels explored themes such as sin and redemption, power and principle, and faith and immorality. His three most famous works are *Crime and Punishment*, *The Brothers Karamazov*, and *The Possessed*. Leo Tolstoy examined the hypocrisy in society and the issue of human suffering in *Anna Karenina*. His other major novel, *War and Peace*, is an epic of Russian life and Russia's struggle against France during the Napoleonic Wars. One of its major themes concerns the driving forces in history.

The publication in 1880 of *The Brothers Karamazov*, Dostoyevsky's last major novel, marked the end of Russia's golden age of literature. However, it was followed in the late nineteenth and early twentieth centuries by another creative era called the "silver age of Russian culture." The outstanding playwright and short-story writer of the golden age was Anton Chekhov (1860-1904). His pessimism and uncompromising realism coexisted with the great sympathy he had for the people he wrote about. His plays *The Seagull, Uncle Vanya*, and *The Cherry Orchard* are still favorites with audiences in Russia and around the world. Chekhov's short stories remain among the best ever written in any language. Andrei Bely (1880–1934), Aleksandr Blok (1880-1921), and Maxim Gorky (1868–1936) were among the many other brilliant talents of the silver age.

Osip Mandelstam (1891–1938) and Anna Akhmatova (1889–1966) were brilliant poets whose lives spanned the tsarist and Soviet eras. Like so many other writers and intellectuals, both suffered horribly under Stalin. Mandelstam died in a Soviet labor camp. Yevgeny Zamiatin (1884–1937), author of the novel *WE*, was fortunate to be allowed to emigrate from the Soviet Union in 1932. He joined other exiled writers such as Ivan Bunin (1870–1954), the first Russian to win the Nobel Prize for literature (in 1933). The next Russian to win that prize was Boris Pasternak (1890–1960), who received it in 1958. He was brutally hounded by Soviet authorities for daring to have his novel *Dr. Zhivago* published abroad because Soviet censors would not allow it to be published at home. Another brilliant writer whose career was partially crippled by censorship was Mikhail Bulgakov (1891–1940). His greatest work, *The Master and the Margarita*, was not published until the mid-1960s. At that time, only excerpts were published in Russia, while a more complete version appeared in the West. Aleksandr Solzhenitsyn (1918–) was the outstanding Russian author of the second half of the twentieth century.

Lucinschi, Petru K. (1940–)

President of Moldova. A career Communist Party official during the Soviet era, Lucinschi implemented Mikhail Gorbachev's perestroika policies while serving as Moldova's Communist Party leader in 1989. He became chairman of the Moldovan parliament after Moldova achieved independence and was elected president over incumbent Mircha Snegur in December 1996. During the election campaign Lucinschi presented himself as a democratic and reformist alternative to his rival who would work to end the political and ethnic divisions that plague Moldova.

Lukashenko, Aleksandr (1954–)

President of Belarus, elected overwhelmingly in July 1994. Only thirty-nine years old when he swept to victory over a former Communist, Lukashenko ran on a platform filled with wild promises and threats that appealed to a population wearied by corruption and hard times. A specialist in agriculture and former manager of a collective farm who supported the anti-Gorbachev coup of August 1991, the eccentric Lukashenko promised to promote union with Russia, put his election opponent in prison, and halt privatization (which had not gone very far in Belarus). His outlandish remarks led some people to call him the "Belarusian Zhirinovsky." One expert commented that Lukashenko had "no ideology....no program...[and] no economic or political background."[11] True to his word, Lukashenko worked hard to promote political and economic ties between Russia and Belarus. In 1996 Lukashenko was able to push through a new constitution that greatly expanded his powers.

Luzhkov, Yury M. (1936–)

Controversial Mayor of Moscow since 1992. Luzhkov served as Moscow's vice-mayor under Gavril Popov from 1991 to 1992. He is a close ally of Boris Yeltsin and a tough politician. As the undisputed boss of his country's largest and most important city, Luzhkov is considered a potential presidential candidate when Yeltsin passes from the scene.

Mafia

Since 1991 organized crime has become Russia's most serious problem. By mid-1990 there were more than 5,000 criminal organizations or gangs in Russia, about 500 in Moscow alone. Borrowing a term used to describe organized crime in Italy and the United States, Russians refer to these gangs as "mafias." Many Russian mafias have their roots in the late Soviet era, when, under Brezhnev, corruption reached into the highest levels of Soviet bureaucracy. By the mid-1990s Russian criminal organizations engaged in a vast array of illegal activities and controlled a large part of the country's new private economy and legal businesses. They often settled their scores in deadly shootouts in broad daylight on the main streets of Russia's large cities. Their list of murder victims included government officials and foreign business people. Russia's mafia gangs used their vast resources to bribe underpaid police. They are considered a serious threat not only to individuals but to Russia's struggling democracy itself. Mafia gangs are also active and constitute a major problem in Ukraine and other post-Soviet states.

Maskhadov, Aslan (1951–)

President of Chechnya. Maskhadov was born in Kazakhstan, where his parents were deported with the rest of the Chechen people by Stalin during World War II. He reached Chechnya with his parents at the age of six, when the Chechens were allowed to return to their homeland after Stalin's death. Maskhadov became a career solider in the Soviet army before returning to Chechnya in 1991 to become head of the Chechen armed forces under President Djohar Dudaev. He led those forces to victory over the Russian army in fighting that lasted from 1994 to 1996. Maskhadov established a reputation for steely nerve both as a military commander and negotiator, a man prepared to be flexible on some issues while remaining steadfast in his pursuit of Chechen independence. He won a decisive victory in Chechnya's first presidential elections in January 1997. He now faces the dual tasks of rebuilding his war-ravaged homeland and leading Chechnya to complete independence, a goal that still faces strong opposition from Moscow.

Meri, Lennart (1929–)

President of Estonia. Meri's family background helped him win election as his country's president. His father was an important official during Estonia's short period of independence after World War I. As a young boy, Meri was deported with his father to Siberia. People still ask how his father gained his release from Siberian exile in 1945, at a time when so many Estonians were being arrested and sent there.

Also, as an official of the Soviet Writers' Union, Meri cooperated with Soviet authorities, while at the same time trying to defend Estonian culture. He is the author of a major work about Estonian prehistory. Prior to becoming Estonia's president, Meri served as its foreign minister. He was reelected to a second term as president in 1996.

Mikhailov, Nikita S. (1945–)

Celebrated Russian film director. Mikhailov's film *Burnt by the Sun* won the 1995 Academy Award for best foreign film. The film traces the fate of a family during the 1930s and graphically portrays the horrors of those years under Stalin. Mikhailov played one of the leading roles, that of a Russian general, while his wife and young daughter played the general's wife and daughter in the film. Mikhailov himself comes from a privileged Communist background, and although his film bitterly attacks Stalin, it has been criticized for being too forgiving of those who collaborated with Stalin. Although he holds strongly nationalistic views and greatly dislikes Yeltsin, Mikhailov supported the government in the last election because, he said, there "was no other choice. We can't afford to go back."[12]

Minsk

Capital and largest city of Belarus (population: 1.6 million). Minsk was a large and well-known city in 1154 when the famous Arab traveler Abu Abdallah Muhamed put it on his map of the world. Since then Minsk has survived destruction or damage at the hands of a long list of foreign invaders, including the Crimean Tatars in 1505, the French in 1812, the Germans in 1918, the Poles in 1919–1920, and especially the Nazi Germans during World War II. Minsk lost half its population in World War II, about the same proportion that was Jewish before the war began.

During the twentieth century Minsk and its surroundings were a killing ground even before the Germans got there. In 1988, a mass grave containing an estimated 100,000 bodies, all victims of Stalin's purges of the 1930s, was discovered in the Kuropaty Forest outside the city. Other sites may bring the total number of victims buried near Minsk to an astounding 900,000.

Today a few of Minsk's old wooden buildings remain standing, and several old churches and cathedrals have been completely or partially restored. However, most of Minsk is a city almost entirely rebuilt in the Soviet style. Fortunately, postwar Soviet planners included many parks and attractive avenues that gave Minsk a more favorable appearance than many other Soviet cities. Minsk's population tripled between 1945 and 1991, as the Soviet regime turned the city into an industrial center.

Minsk was the site of two pivotal meetings in the history of the Soviet Union. In 1898 a group of Marxist revolutionaries gathered in Minsk to found the Russian Social Democratic Party, one of whose factions became the Bolshevik Party in 1903. That meeting thereby set in motion key forces that led to the establishment of the Soviet Union. In December 1991, Boris Yeltsin of Russia, Leonid Kravchuk of Ukraine, and Stanislav Shushkevich of Belarus met there and founded the Commonwealth of Independent States. That meeting completed the process that led to the dissolution of the Soviet Union.

Moscow

The capital, largest city (population: 9 million), and, according to popular sentiments, the "soul" of Russia. Moscow is also the former capital of the Soviet Union. The first mention of the city dates from 1147, when Moscow was a small collection of wooden huts on the banks of the Moskva River. Nine years later the Kievian Prince Yuri Dolgoruky arrived in Moscow and ordered that a fort—a *kremlin* in Russian—be built. The wooden kremlin did not prevent the city from being burned and destroyed in 1237 during the Mongol invasion. Although one of Moscow's fourteenth-century princes surrounded the city with stone walls, the Tatars burned the city many times during the next 250 years. The last Tatar assault on Moscow occurred in 1571, during the reign of Ivan the Terrible. They burned the entire city except for the Kremlin, which by then already had the massive stone walls that still surround it today. The city's last great fire occurred in 1812, when it burned to the ground after being occupied by Napoleon.

The building and rebuilding of Moscow is most closely associated with three of Russia's great tyrants: Ivan the Great, Ivan the Terrible, and Stalin. Ivan the Great hired Italian architects and rebuilt the Kremlin by adding new walls and towers and three cathedrals. Ivan the Terrible, also using Italian architects, built the magnificent St. Basil's Cathedral, a unique combination of nine churches, famous for its brilliant colors and onion-shaped domes. According to legend, Ivan blinded his architects when they finished their work so they could never again build anything so beautiful. Ivan's building projects also determined the shape of Red Square, Moscow's huge central plaza. Stalin demolished many of old Moscow's landmarks, including the famous Cathedral of Christ the Savior, and rebuilt much of the city according to one of the world's first urban plans. Some of his projects, in particular seven enormous skyscrapers known as "Stalin's Wedding Cakes," have become symbols for the massive ugliness and inhuman scale of Soviet-era buildings. Stalin also was responsible for the Moscow Metro, one of the world's finest and most beautiful subway systems. The Metro was built in the 1930s at breakneck speed without regard for the lives of the project's workers, many of whom died from the harsh working conditions or in accidents.

After World War II, especially during the Khrushchev era, Moscow experienced a building spree. Huge housing proj-

The Kremlin, left, and St. Basil's Cathedral

ects were built in outlying areas. Because they were poorly constructed many of the buildings deteriorated within a few years. The people called the buildings *khrushchoby*, a play on the name Khrushchev and the word *trushchoby*, which means "slums" in Russian.

There is one notable part of Moscow that few people have seen; it is an underground city about 4 miles (6 kilometers) from Red Square. Built during the Brezhnev era, the 500-acre (200-hectare) complex has several levels, streets wide enough for cars, and its own Metro. It also has its own movie theaters, swimming pools, and other conveniences. Moscow's underground city is a Cold War relic; it was built to house 30,000 Soviet leaders for up to thirty years in the event of nuclear war.

Today the core of Moscow still remains Red Square, St. Basil's Cathedral, and the Kremlin. The massive Kremlin, still the seat of the Russian government, dominates the area.

Its red brick walls have a circumference of 1.5 miles (2.4 kilometers). They are 10 to 20 feet (3 to 6 kilometers) thick, 65 feet (20 meters) high in some places, and reinforced by twenty towers. Yet the Kremlin, seemingly and deceptively unchanging over the centuries, stands face-to-face with symbols of change. Directly in front of its walls, fronting Red Square, is the squat Lenin Mausoleum, where the long-dead Bolshevik leader's embalmed body lies for the admiring and curious to view. On October 6, 1993, two days after defeating the coup against him, President Boris Yeltsin ended the changing of the guard at the Communist shrine, a ritual that had taken place every hour on the hour—except during World War II—for sixty-nine years. Across Red Square the huge GUM department store, for decades a bastion of socialist shopping, has become a giant capitalist mall. In place of the old stalls selling the dreary wares of Soviet central planning, there are privately run shops selling everything from Russian-made products to luxury goods from all over the world.

Moscow is a metropolis of striking contrasts and dramatic changes. In fact, if you go to Moscow you will need an up-to-date map, since the names of so many of its streets and landmarks have been changed since 1991. Moscow's traditional landmarks—from the Kremlin and St. Basil's to the Bolshoi Theater (home of the world-famous Bolshoi Ballet), the Tratyakov Gallery (which houses many of the world's great art masterpieces, an outstanding collection of pre-Revolutionary Russian art, and the world's best collection of Russian religious icons), Gorky Park, and the Metropol Hotel—are still there. At the same time, the city has become a capitalist hotbed, with new housing, soaring real estate prices, new banks and businesses, and growing numbers of both rich and poor. It is also the center of the dangerous crime wave that has swept Russia. If Moscow is indeed Russia's soul, then it shows better than anything else the challenge that Russia faces to preserve the best of its past while adapting to meet a changing future.

Nazarbayev, Nursultan A.
(1940–)

President of Kazakhstan. Nazarbayev began his working life as a steelworker and later became a respected economist. He was put in charge of Kazakhstan by Mikhail Gorbachev in 1989 and became his country's leader upon its independence. It was in large part due to Nazarbayev's efforts that a second meeting to establish the Commonwealth of Independent States (CIS), which allowed Kazakhstan and ten other Soviet republics to become founding members, was held in Almaty on December 21, 1991. Although he rules in an authoritarian manner, Nazarbayev has earned a reputation as a moderate and sensible politician. He has worked hard to guarantee the rights of non-Kazakhs, especially ethnic Russians, in Kazakhstan and won praise for agreeing to give up Kazakhstan's nuclear weapons. Nazarbayev also has had considerable success in attracting foreign investment in Kazakhstan to develop its oil and natural gas resources. In 1994 he met with U.S. President Bill Clinton in Washington and received promises of foreign aid.

Near Abroad

The term used by Russians to designate the other fourteen countries of the former Soviet Union. Its use usually implies the belief that Russia has the right to a special influence in the region, even to the point of interfering in the internal affairs of the countries involved.

Nemstov, Boris (1961–)

First Deputy Prime Minister, formerly governor of Nizhny Novgorod region and a leading economic reformer. He was the driving force behind the unusually successful reform and privatization efforts in the city of Nizhny Novgorod. A physicist by training, during the Soviet era Nemstov dared to meet with dissident Andrei Sakharov when the latter was under house arrest. He also led a successful effort to block the construction of a nuclear power plant near Nizhny Novgorod that he believed was unsafe.

Niyazov, Saparmurad A. (1940–)

President of Turkmenistan. Niyazov rules his country in the dictatorial fashion of an old-fashioned sultan. He is called "Turkmenbashi," or leader of the Turkmen. His *Sayings of Turkmenbashi*, collected into a little book, are memorized by students at all schools and universities. Niyazov's picture is everywhere. Government officials, who wear gold pins of his profile, often kiss Niyazov's jeweled hand when greeting him. While most of his people live in poverty, the Leader of the Turkmen, who has said "All I wanted was a small cozy house," is having a $100 million gold-domed presidential palace built for his use.[13] It will join several other palaces and mansions that Niyazov now enjoys. What do ordinary Turkmen think of all this? As one melon farmer, whose small hut contains the obligatory portrait of Turkmenbashi, put it, "It is wiser not to speak."[14]

Nizhny Novgorod

City about 250 miles (400 kilometers) east of Moscow, where successful economic reform efforts have been led by Boris

Nemtsov. Nizhny Novgorod, founded in 1221 at the point where the Volga and Oka rivers meet, has a long tradition of commerce and business. A Russian proverb says that "St. Petersburg is the brain, Moscow the soul, and Nizhny Novgorod the pocketbook of Russia." During the Soviet era Nizhny Novgorod (then called Gorky, after the famed pro-Bolshevik writer) was a closed city because of its top-secret military factories.

Novosibirsk

Largest city in Siberia (population: 1.5 million). Novosibirsk was founded in 1893 during the building of the Trans-Siberian Railway. During the 1920s it was greatly expanded and turned into an industrial and transportation center. In typical Soviet fashion, it was built to serve its economic functions without concern for the quality of life of its inhabitants. During the Khrushchev era a new suburb, called Akademgorodok, was built about 18 miles (29 kilometers) south of the city. It was designed as a major research center and provided with superior housing, consumer goods, and cultural facilities in order to attract topflight people. Akademgorodok was an idea that worked for about three decades. About 65,000 specialists and their families lived there. It had twenty-three prestigious institutes working in the sciences and social sciences. However, the Russian government has been unable to support these institutes, and many of their employees have moved elsewhere in search of work.

NTV

During the Soviet era, all media were controlled by the state. That has changed. Privately owned television is spreading rapidly in Russia and challenging state-owned stations to improve their programming and management. Both NTV and a network called TV6 are moving toward becoming national networks as they add stations throughout Russia. One sign of the importance of privately owned television stations has been the reporting on the Chechnya war. The government was angered by NTV's independent reporting that gave the public information about how badly the war was going. Their reporting forced the huge state-run Ostankino network to deliver a more balanced, less progovernment account of the war. As one expert put it, the development of independent television is "one of the most positive outcomes in the development of Russia after the end of the Soviet Union.[15]

Odessa

Ukraine's fourth-largest city and most important port. Odessa was founded in the 1790s on land conquered from Turkey. As a major port, the city long has been a meeting place of different cultures. Like so many cities in the western part of the former Soviet Union, Odessa has survived great hardship but has always managed to recover. It is a popular health resort with more than 25 miles (40 kilometers) of beaches along its Black Sea coast. Its people take pride in inventing the country's funniest jokes and writing its most popular songs. Today it appears shabby and neglected, but its people seem to have kept their upbeat approach to life.

Pamfilova, Ella (1953–)

Member of the Russian Duma and former Russian Federation minister of social security. Since she entered politics in 1989, Pamfilova has made it her mission to help the millions of her fellow citizens who have been hurt by the wrenching process of Russia's economic change. She was appointed to her ministerial post in 1991, but resigned in 1994 in protest against the government's failure to provide Russia's elderly and other poor with a decent social safety net. She has continued to serve as a Duma deputy. Pamfilova's staunch advocacy of the poor and helpless has given her a national reputation. Each day she receives letters from citizens in need who know that she is one political figure who is prepared to fight for them.

Podnieks, Juris (1951–1992)

Latvian filmmaker. In 1987, his documentary film *Is It Easy to Be Young?* earned him admiration at home and awards abroad. The film revealed the alienation and despair of a whole generation of Soviet young people, including veterans of the Afghanistan war. Podnieks also made other dramatic documentaries, including some that involved great risks. He was the only cameraman to film the destroyed Chernobyl nuclear plant (from both the air and ground) and was on the scene in January 1991, first in Vilnius and a week later in Riga, when Soviet troops attacked local government buildings. Among those killed in Riga was Podnieks's cameraman. His courageous films made Podnieks a hero to fellow Latvians. The country mourned when he died in a scuba-diving accident in 1992 at the age of forty-one.

Political Parties (Russia)

During the Soviet era there was only one political party in Russia and the other republics: the Communist Party of the Soviet Union (CPSU). It had a membership of more than 20 million people. Since 1991, political parties have formed, disintegrated, and reformed in rapid succession. What follows is a list of the most significant political parties in the Russian Federation as of the December 1995 elections, with the percentage of votes they received in the proportional representation race and their total seats in parliament.[16]

Communist Party of the Russian Federation (CPRF) (22.3%, 157 seats) is by far the most successful of the Communist groupings formed from the rubble of the CPSU. The party has a membership of about 580,000, far larger than any other Russian political party. It is led by Gennadi Zyuganov. Svetlana Gorycheva, a former Soviet prosecutor from Vladivostok, is one of the few women among the party's leadership. She first made her mark in Russian politics in 1991 as a bitter opponent of Boris Yeltsin in the Russian parliament.

Our Home Is Russia (10.13%, 55 seats) is a centrist group led by Viktor Chernomyrdin.

Yalboko (6.89%, 45 seats), led by Grigory Yavlinsky, was the strongest reformist party in the 1995 election.

Liberal Democratic Party (LDP) (11.18%, 51 seats) is the extreme nationalist group led by Vladimir Zhirinovsky.

Congress of Russian Communities (KRO) (4.31%, 5 seats) is a nationalist group led by Yuri Skokov.

Agrarian Party (3.78%, 20 seats) is a close ally of the CPRF.

Russia's Democratic Choice (3.86%, 9 seats) is the reformist party led by Yegor Gaidar.

Women of Russia (4.61%, 3 seats) combines its concern for women's interests with sympathy for traditional Communist concerns. Its leader is a former secondary-school science teacher and Communist official named Alevtina Fedulova.

Russian Communist Worker's Party (4.53%, 1 seat) is a hard-line Communist party. The party, headed by Viktor Tyulkin, is made up of diehard Stalinists who accuse Gennadi Zyuganov and the CPRF of being too moderate. It is important, despite winning only one seat in a single-seat district, because it received the sixth greatest number of votes in the proportional representation race (5 percent was needed to win seats in parliament). The party's best-known figure is Viktor Anpilov, a fiery speaker who supported the October 1993 uprising against Boris Yeltsin. Another important member is Albert Makashov, a former career soldier and extreme nationalist. Makashov finished last in Russia's 1991 presidential election and was among those arrested at the White House in the October 1993 coup attempt.

Several other parties won a total of twenty-seven seats in the 450-seat Duma, the lower house of the Russian Federation parliament.

Popov, Gavril K. (1936–)
Mayor of Moscow, 1991–1992. Of Greek descent, Popov was an economics professor and early advocate of market reforms. He was elected to the Congress of People's Deputies in 1989 and then to the Moscow City Council. Popov joined Boris Yeltsin in his dramatic resignation from the Communist Party in 1990. He was elected mayor of Moscow in June 1991, but his popularity faded and he resigned the next year.

Primakov, Yevgeny M. (1929–)
Foreign minister of the Russian Federation. Boris Yeltsin appointed Primakov foreign minister in January 1996 to replace Andrei Kozyrev. Primakov's appointment was another indication that Russian foreign policy would be less pro-Western and more nationalistic. As he put it, "Russia was and remains a great power. Her foreign policy should correspond to that status."[17]

Primakov was educated at the Soviet Union's prestigious Institute for Oriental Studies. He is an expert on the Arab world and speaks Arabic fluently. After serving in a variety of positions, Primakov became one of Leonid Brezhnev's most trusted foreign-policy advisers. In 1991, while working for Mikhail Gorbachev, Primakov angered the United States with his last-ditch effort to arrange a face-saving withdrawal from Kuwait for Iraq's Saddam Hussein, an old Primakov acquaintance. As power shifted from Gorbachev to Yeltsin, so did Primakov. As a former colleague put it, "He [Primakov] has no ideology. He's a genuine pragmatist."[18] Before becoming foreign minister, Primakov headed the Foreign Intelligence Service, one of the branches of the former KGB.

Prokhanov, Aleksandr A. (1938–)

Extreme nationalist Russian newspaper editor and novelist. Prokhanov's newspaper, *Zavtra* (Tomorrow), is a monthly that is printed on cheap paper and has a tiny circulation. Yet it has helped make its editor one of the most important journalists in Russia. Prokhanov has used his newspaper to bring together Communists and nationalists of different stripes who oppose Yeltsin, economic reform, and democratic government. Gennadi Zyuganov used Prokhanov's fusion of Communist and nationalist ideas to lead the Communist Party of the Russian Federation to victory in the 1995 parliamentary elections. Prokhanov openly states "I am an anti-democrat."[19] He also is a vicious anti-Semite and bitter critic of the West.

Rakhmonov, Emomali (1952–)

President of Tajikistan. Rakhmonov is a hard-line, formerly high-ranking Communist who has managed to hang on to power with the help of financial and military support from Russia and Uzbekistan. Both countries have supported Rakhmonov and his faction of former Communist Party officials because they fear the spread of Islamic fundamentalism in Central Asia if rebel forces come to power in Tajikistan. Rakhmonov's government is a harsh dictatorship. People who speak out are arrested, and newspapers that dared to criticize the government have been closed and their editors either murdered, jailed, or driven into exile.

Rasputin, Valentin G. (1937–)
Major Russian writer. The Siberian-born Rasputin is one of the best-known so-called "country writers" who advocate a return to Russia's traditional rural values. They also call for protection of Russia's ravaged environment. An outstanding talent, Rasputin has been called "Siberia's Faulkner." However, at times Rasputin's advocacy of Russian values has taken on a distinctly anti-Western and anti-Semitic tone.

Republics: Soviet and Russian Federation
During the Soviet era, the Soviet Union contained two types of republics, both based on national or ethnic identity. There were fifteen Soviet Socialist Republics (SSRs), which were the main divisions of the country as a whole. These Soviet Socialist Republics became the fifteen post-Soviet countries when the Soviet Union collapsed. The Soviet Union also contained twenty so-called "Autonomous Republics." Sixteen of them were within the Russian Soviet Federated Socialist Republic (RSFSR); the rest were in other SSRs. These sixteen autonomous republics became "republics" within the newly independent Russian Federation when the Soviet Union collapsed. One of the republics—Chechen-Ingushetia—split in two, thereby creating a seventeenth republic. When four of the "autonomous regions" of the former RSFSR declared themselves to be "republics," the number of ethnic republics within the Russian Federation reached twenty-one. They accounted for about 28.6 percent of the Russian Federation's territory and about 15 percent of its population. However,

almost half their population was Russian, and Russians in fact made up the majority in nine of these republics.

Riga

Capital and largest city of Latvia (population: 916,000). Riga was founded in 1201 by a German bishop and then turned into a fortress from which German knights conquered the surrounding region. It passed through Polish and Swedish hands before falling under Russian control in 1709 during the reign of Peter the Great. The city developed into a major trading center as a result of its strategic location at the mouth of the Daugava River on the Gulf of Riga and its warm-water port (which means its harbor does not freeze and allows ships to pass in the winter).

While Riga's Latvian population grew as people moved in from the countryside, it still remained less than half Latvian. During the Soviet era Riga became an industrial center. Soviet Russification policies left the city about 70 percent Russian when Latvia regained its independence in late 1991.

Today Riga is the largest and most cosmopolitan city in the Baltic states. Riga is blessed with about 20 miles (32 kilometers) of sandy beaches that have lured tourists for generations. Unfortunately, the Baltic is so polluted that at times swimming has been banned.

Rodionov, Igor (1937–)

Russian Federation defense minister, 1996-1997. A career soldier with a reputation for integrity, Rodionov replaced the fired Pavel Grachev in July 1996. Appointed in large part because of the efforts of Aleksandr Lebed, Rodionov was unpopular in some circles because of his role in the bloody suppression of civilian demonstrators in Georgia's capital of Tbilisi in 1989. Rodionov lined up against Lebed when the latter was fired by President Yeltsin in October 1996. He was dismissed for not making plans to reduce the size of Russia's Military.

Romanov Family

The ruling dynasty of Russia from 1613 to 1917. In 1917 the Romanovs were deposed and the monarchy ended. A little more than a year later the Bolsheviks murdered Nicholas II, his family (his wife Alexandra, four daughters, and a son), and four attendants in Yekaterinburg. The execution was carried out on Lenin's orders. The bodies were then doused with sulfuric acid and buried in an abandoned mine. The house in which they were murdered was destroyed in 1977—the secret order from Moscow was carried out by Boris Yeltsin—in order to prevent it from becoming an anti-Soviet shrine. In 1991 archaeologists excavated the bones of nine people from a shallow pit near Yekaterinburg. Computer analysis, DNA testing, and comparisons to blood and hair samples from living descendants of the tsar show that the bones belonged to the tsar, his wife, and three of their daughters, including Anastasia. That find ended more than six decades of speculation that Anastasia, the youngest daughter, had somehow survived. The Bolshevik records of the killing, long kept secret, indicate that the son and fourth daughter were buried elsewhere.

As of 1996, plans to rebury the bodies in St. Petersburg's Peter and Paul Cathedral had not yet been carried out. However, in 1992 the body of Grand Duke Vladimir Kirillovich Romanov, a descendant of the tsar and heir to the vacant Russian throne, was brought to St. Petersburg and given a formal Orthodox funeral.

Russia: Names
Prior to 1917, the word "Russia" referred to the Russian Empire, the world's largest country, whose population in fact was about half Russian. After 1917 the Russian Empire, minus a few parts of its western fringe, became the Union of Soviet Socialist Republics, or Soviet Union. The largest of the fifteen main divisions of the Soviet Union was the Russian Soviet Federated Socialist Republic (RSFSR). The RSFSR composed about three quarters of the Soviet Union and contained about half its population. It is the RSFSR that became the Russian Federation with the collapse of the Soviet Union.

Russian Orthodox Church
Church to which most Russians traditionally have belonged, associated with Russian national identity for more than 1,000 years. The Russian Orthodox Church has been deeply entwined with Russian history since 988, when Prince Vladimir of Kiev made the Eastern Orthodox version of Christianity (based in Constantinople) the religion of his realm. The Church survived more than seven decades of antireligious Soviet pressure and propaganda and had about 50 million believers when the Soviet Union collapsed in 1991. It has been enjoying a strong revival since the Gorbachev era. Thousands of churches and monasteries have been returned to church control since the fall of the Soviet Union. By 1993,

there were about 20,000 Orthodox churches in Russia, versus 7,000 in 1988. (In 1917, when the Bolsheviks came to power, there were about 50,000.) Between 1991 and 1996, the number of parishes in Moscow alone grew from 50 to 200.

Many Orthodox priests have condemned the spread of Western values in Russia. They assert that those values have led to violence and moral decline. At the same time, there are divisions within the Church. Some members of its clergy want the Church to break with Russian tradition and establish real independence from the state. They also would like to see more room for different opinions within the Church. More traditional clergymen want a return to pre-Revolutionary status, with the Church as Russia's national religion and closely tied to the state.

Rutskoi, Aleksandr V. (1942–)

Russian Federation vice president, 1991–1993, and former Yeltsin ally who became his bitter foe. An air force general and Afghanistan war hero, Rutskoi was a supporter of reform during the Gorbachev era. He was elected Russia's vice president as Yeltsin's running mate in June 1991 and helped organize the defense of the Russian White House during the August 1991 coup. However, within a few months after the collapse of the Soviet Union, Rutskoi, who considered himself a moderate conservative and nationalist, split with Yeltsin. He strongly opposed Yeltsin's economic reforms and called Yegor Gaidar and his youthful colleagues "boys in pink shorts."[20] He also warned that democracy was unsuited to Russia at a time when it needed "law and order." Along with Ruslan Khasbulatov, Rutskoi led the October 1993 coup attempt against Yeltsin and was proclaimed Russia's acting president by the Khasbulatov-led parliament. Rutskoi was imprisoned when the coup failed, but was pardoned and released in February 1994 when the parliament issued an amnesty to all participants in the August 1991 and October 1993 coups. He began a political comeback in impressive fashion in 1996 when he was elected governor of Russia's Kursk region in a landslide.

Rybkin, Ivan P. (1946–)
Head of Russia's National Security Council and former speaker of the Russian parliament (1994–1995). An engineer by training, Rybkin was elected to parliament in 1993 as a member of the Agrarian Party, a group closely allied with the Communist Party of the Russian Federation led by Gennadi Zyuganov. In the contest for speaker, he also had the support of the extreme nationalist Liberal Democratic Party led by Vladimir Zhirinovsky. However, once in office Rybkin proved to be surprisingly moderate and often cooperated with Prime Minister Viktor Chernomyrdin. As a result, after the 1995 parliamentary elections Chernomyrdin's moderate Our Home Is Russia party supported Rybkin's unsuccessful bid to be reelected speaker. In October 1996 he was appointed head of Russia's National Security Council to replace the fired Aleksandr Lebed. His most important and difficult assignment will be dealing with Chechnya.

St. Petersburg
Russia's second-largest city, known as the "Venice of the North" because of its many canals and great beauty. It is built on more than a hundred islands where the Neva River reaches the Gulf of Finland in an area that once was largely swampland. There was, however, no beauty in building the city that Peter the Great called his "window on the west." Thousands of peasants conscripted to work on the project died working under terrible conditions in the swampland. They called Russia's new capital the "city built on bones."

Peter's city has had three official names. It was called St. Petersburg from its founding until 1914. In response to the anti-German mood in Russia after the outbreak of World War I, the German-sounding St. Petersburg was changed to the Russian Petrograd. In 1924, after Lenin's death, the city's name became Leningrad. In 1991 the Russian parliament officially changed the name back to St. Petersburg. Through all the political storms and name changes, generations of people who live there have affectionately called their city "Peter."

Since its founding almost three hundred years ago, St. Petersburg has survived floods, the Nazi 900-day siege that killed 800,000 civilians, and the Communists, who changed its name to Leningrad and moved Russia's capital to Moscow. More than any single event, the siege of the city by the Nazis and the heroic resistance by St. Petersburg's citizens is a symbol of the city's pride and the unity of its people across generations. A simple poem etched into a concrete slab in a cemetery where uncounted thousands of wartime dead lie sums up that spirit:

Their names we cannot list,
so many they are
who lie under the eternal guard of granite
But know who hear this:
no one is forgotten
nothing is forgotten.[21]

During the nineteenth and twentieth centuries, St. Petersburg was the center of modern Russian culture. Great nineteenth-century writers like Aleksandr Pushkin and Fyodor Dostoyevsky set some of their most important works in St. Petersburg. In the early twentieth century, Anna Pavlova and Vaslav Nijinsky, Russia's greatest ballet dancers in their day, called the city their home. Today St. Petersburg remains a great cultural and industrial center. It is the home to one of the world's most distinguished ballet companies, many theaters, and more than sixty museums, including the world-famous Hermitage. Lying 60 degrees north of the equator, at the same latitude as southern Alaska, St. Petersburg is known for its "White Nights," a period of about three weeks each summer when the sun never sets. Night is replaced by a twilight that bathes the city in a whitish glow for about 30 to 40 minutes. St. Petersburg celebrates its White Nights with a music and arts festival.

In certain ways St. Petersburg was fortunate that in 1918 Communists abandoned it as their capital. While large parts of Moscow's old historic center were demolished and rebuilt in dreary Soviet style, St. Petersburg's center, including the ornate mansions and the rest of the 15,000 historic buildings that line its avenues and canals, were spared, although not maintained either. The director of the St. Petersburg Cultural Fund observed, "The city was simply transported in its entirety into our era, albeit worse for wear."[22]

Since 1991, there has been new development, with new stores, hotels, and restaurants opening up behind the facades of fine old buildings on streets like the Nevsky Prospekt, the city's main avenue. Now a major concern among the residents is that development does not overwhelm "Peter's" traditional beauty and grace. As the head of the city's historic preservation department put it, "The issue here is maintaining a high level of culture."[23]

Samarkand

Uzbekistan's second-largest city. With a population of about 400,000, Samarkand has a largely Tajik population and is a source of contention between Uzbekistan and Tajikistan.

Sometimes called Uzbekistan's "golden city," Samarkand already was a famous walled city when conquered by Alexander the Great in 329 B.C. Alexander was deeply impressed by what he saw. Samarkand apparently also stimulated his imagination, for shortly after leaving the city Alexander proclaimed himself a god. Samarkand was one of the main stops along the fabled Silk Road, which for centuries linked China with the Middle East and Europe. In the fourteenth century the conqueror Tamerlane made Samarkand the capital of his empire. Tamerlane brought artists from all over his vast empire to the city to build many beautiful monuments that visitors still admire today.

In the 1920s, despite its largely Tajik population, Samarkand was made part of Uzbekistan by Stalin as part of his policy of "divide and rule." Today Samarkand's center, with its mosques and bazaar, reflects the city's exotic past, while the modern city outside is built in the sterile Soviet style. Samarkand's focal point remains a remarkable complex called the Registan ("Place of Sand"). Built over a period of 250 years beginning in the early 1400s, it is a huge plaza framed by three beautifully tiled buildings that once housed Islamic seminaries.

Secessionist Regions and Rebellions

Several of the post-Soviet states, including Russia, have faced secessionist rebellions since 1991. The Armenian majority of Nagorno-Karabakh wants to secede from Azerbaijan and unite with Armenia. In Russia the secessionist rebellion in Chechnya has led to terrible destruction. Georgia faces two armed secessionist movements, in Abkhazia and in South Ossetia. Moldova faces Russian and Ukrainian secessionists in the Trans-Dniester region. [See chapters on each country for additional details.]

Seleznev, Gennadi (1947–)

Speaker of Russian parliament, elected January 1996. Seleznev's election as speaker came after the victory of the Zyuganov-led CPRF in the 1995 parliamentary elections. Seleznev worked his way up through the ranks of the defunct Communist Party of the Soviet Union. He became editor of its newspaper *Pravda* in 1991, remaining on its editorial board after his election as speaker. Most of Seleznev's backing in the contest for speaker came from fellow Communists, the Agrarian Party, and other antireform conservative and nationalist forces. His election reflected the weakness of reformers and even centrists in the post-1995 Russian parliament.

Shevardnadze, Eduard A. (1928–)

President of Georgia and former foreign minister of the Soviet Union. Aside from Mikhail Gorbachev, no man is more closely associated with the end of the Cold War than Eduard Shevardnadze. Like Gorbachev, Shevardnadze was a long-time Communist official and political boss. He headed the Georgian Communist Party from 1972 to 1985, building a solid reputation as a foe of corruption. Shevardnadze left Georgia for Moscow in 1985 when Gorbachev chose him to be his foreign minister. He became one of Gorbachev's closest and most trusted advisers. But Shevardnadze resigned in December 1990 because he believed that Gorbachev was straying from the path of reform. At that time, Shevardnadze warned of growing hard-line Communist opposition to both Gorbachev and reform, which included the dramatic and urgent sentences: "The reformers have headed for the hills. Dictatorship is coming."[24] Less than nine months later, Communist Party die-hards launched their coup against Gorbachev.

Shevardnadze became president of Georgia in 1992. In 1993, Georgia's mounting problems drove him to resign. Shevardnadze told Georgia's parliament, "I'm fed up with it all,"[25] but returned to office when the parliament rejected his resignation by a vote of 149 to 0. Overwhelmingly reelected Georgia's president in November 1995, Shevardnadze presides over a deeply troubled and fractured nation.

Shushkevich, Stanislav S. (1934–)

First leader of independent Belarus. Prior to entering politics, Shushkevich had a distinguished career as an engineer in the electronics industry and as a professor of physics. In December 1991, as president of the Supreme Soviet of Belarus, Shushkevich met with Boris Yeltsin and Leonid Kravchuk to set up the Commonwealth of Independent States (CIS). Known as a liberal and a reformer, Shushkevich battled with a Communist-dominated parliament in 1992–1993 in an unsuccessful effort to implement economic reform. In January 1994, the Belarus parliament dismissed Shushkevich from office.

Siberia

Siberia, while only a part of Russia, is the size of a continent. Its name, taken from a Mongolian word, means "sleeping land." Siberia stretches west to east from the Ural Mountains to the Pacific Ocean and south to north from the borders of Kazakhstan, Mongolia, and China to the Arctic Ocean. It covers about 5 million square miles (13 million square kilometers), larger than the United States (with Alaska) and all of western and central Europe combined.

Everything associated with Siberia, it seems, is superlative. Its forests are the largest in the world. Lake Baikal, its largest lake, holds more water than any lake in the world. The Ob River in western Siberia, 3,362 miles (5,410 kilometers) long, is the longest in Russia and the fourth-longest river in the world. (Siberia's Lena and Yenisey rivers rank ninth and thirteenth, respectively.) Siberia's reserves of oil and natural gas, as well as many minerals including gold and diamonds, are among the world's most extensive. The Trans-Siberian railroad that crosses the region is by far the longest in the world. And the beautiful Siberian tiger, which has been hunted to the brink of extinction, is the world's largest cat.

The Siberian town of Oimyakon, where the temperature drops to -94 degrees Fahrenheit (-70°C) in winter, is probably the coldest inhabited place on Earth. During Siberia's short summers, grasses in some regions grow 3 inches (76 millimeters) per day in their struggle to take advantage of precious moments of heat and light.

Neither numbers nor maps can satisfactorily convey the vastness of Siberia. A poem by a local resident about the region's enormous forest, or taiga, does a better job:

> The taiga is a universe without an end
> Those that live within it are the stars
> Bright stars are the eyes of the beasts.
> The space between the stars is infinite
> For the taiga is a universe without end.[26]

The Russian conquest of Siberia began in the 1580s when a band of Cossacks, under the leadership of a former convict named Yermak, crossed the Ural Mountains and moved eastward. Within sixty years, Russian explorers and fur trappers had reached the Bering Sea. Behind them came the tsar's officials and soldiers. The small groups of native peoples in the region were unable to resist Russian expansion, and they often were treated with great brutality. Eventually they would become a small minority of the population of Siberia.

A major step in the settling of Siberia and exploiting its resources was the building of the Trans-Siberian Railroad. Most of it was completed between 1891 and 1903. Beginning in the 1930s, the Soviet regime pushed large-scale industrialization in the region. A major mining and manufacturing center was developed in western Siberia in the Kuznetsk basin, or Kuzbass, near the city of Novosibirsk. At the same time, vast stretches of Siberia became sites for Stalin's labor camps, where millions of people died.

The settling and exploitation of Siberia continued after Stalin's death. One terrible result, as almost everywhere else in the former Soviet Union, is pollution and environmental destruction on an enormous scale. The damage includes pollution of water and land from nuclear wastes. The Norilsk smelter complex in central Siberia may be the single largest source of air pollution in the entire world. Oil production and leaking pipelines have added to the environmental damage. In the post-Soviet era, a joint Russian-Japanese logging operation stripped the trees from so much land that the bare spots are large enough to be seen from space.

Like the rest of Russia, Siberia's future is very much in doubt. Environmentalists have joined with many people in Siberia who are trying to protect the region from further harm. Their goal is to make sure that Siberia's natural resources are used without destroying its unique and fragile environment. As early as the beginning of the nineteenth century, Russians living in Siberia developed a sense of their own identity. They saw themselves as Russians, to be sure, but also as Siberians. That sense of identity has grown. In the late twentieth century it has been powerfully expressed by a number of popular Siberian-born writers such as Valentin Rasputin. One of their themes is the beauty of nature and protection of the environment. Siberians will need their commitment, and that of Russia's government in far away Moscow, in order to heal from its wounds and prosper.

Snegur, Mircha I. (1940–)
President of Moldova, 1990–1996. Snegur became president of Moldova during the last years of the Gorbachev era and continued in that post during his country's first five years of independence. A career Communist Party official during the Soviet era, he served in a variety of agricultural posts for twenty years. During Snegur's presidency, Moldova's unity was undermined by internal ethnic  turmoil and foreign pressures. He chose to cope with these problems by allying himself with nationalist pro-Romanian groups and becoming increasingly dictatorial in his rule. In December 1996 Mircha Snegur was defeated in his attempt to win reelection by Petru Lucinschi, another former Communist Party official.

Sobchak, Anatoly A. (1937–)
Mayor of St. Petersburg, 1990–1996. In August 1991, while Boris Yeltsin defied the anti-Gorbachev plotters in Moscow, 400 miles (640 kilometers) away Mayor Anatoly Sobchak was standing firm in St. Petersburg (at the time still known as Leningrad). He defied the military commander and personally ordered Soviet troops to stay in their barracks. He thereby stopped them, almost singlehandedly, from occupying the city. Some people call Sobchak the "second hero" of the August 1991 coup.

Sobchak entered politics after a career as a lawyer and law professor. In 1989 he was elected to the Congress of People's Deputies, the new Soviet parliament set up by Mikhail Gorbachev. He was elected mayor of Leningrad in the spring of 1990. By 1996 he had lost support because of hard economic times, a decrease in city services, and several corruption scandals. He was defeated for reelection by Vladimir Yakovlev, a "fresh face" who portrayed himself as a "hands-on" manager capable of restoring city services.

Sobir, Bozor (unknown)
Tajik poet whose fate symbolizes his country's difficulties since independence. Prior to 1991, Sobir wrote poems in which he supported Tajikistan's independence. However, after independence he was charged with antigovernment activity and jailed by the dictatorial Rakhmonov government. A colleague sadly pointed out how Sobir had fought for independence, but after it was achieved "he sits in jail."[27]

Solzhenitsyn, Aleksandr I. (1918–)
Russia's leading twentieth-century novelist and fearless Brezhnev-era dissident. Solzhenitsyn served as an artillery officer in World War II. He was sentenced to seven years in a prison camp for mocking Stalin in a letter intercepted by the police. Solzhenitsyn worked as a mathematics teacher after his release. His first major work was a short novella, *A Day in the Life of Ivan Denisovich*, which portrayed the brutal conditions in Stalin's labor camps. It was published in 1962 during the reformist Khrushchev era. The two masterpieces that fol-

lowed, *The First Circle* and *The Cancer Ward*, had to be smuggled out of the Soviet Union to the West for publication. In 1970, Solzhenitsyn was awarded the Nobel Prize for literature. By then he was an outcast in the Soviet Union. However, he stood his ground firmly and openly denounced the Soviet regime. In 1973 he published the first of his three-volume *The Gulag Archipelago*, a devastating exposé of the Soviet labor camp system that traced its origins back to the earliest days of the Soviet state. He was expelled from the Soviet Union in 1974.

Solzhenitsyn spent the next twenty years in exile, mostly in the United States. He worked on a series of novels collectively called *The Red Wheel*. In his writings on current issues, Solzhenitsyn revealed that he was no fan of Western culture or democracy. He criticized the West as overly materialistic and permissive. He called on Russia to return to its Orthodox roots and peasant traditions. He advocated an authoritarian form of government that he said would best see to the needs of the Russian people. Solzhenitsyn also urged that Russia shed the non-Slavic parts of its empire and form a state with Ukraine and Belarus. In 1994, three years after the collapse of the regime he so bitterly and bravely opposed, Solzhenitsyn returned to Russia to live.

Space Program
Russian interest in spaceflight goes back to the nineteenth century. The practical study of spaceflight dates from 1903, when a physics and mathematics teacher named Konstantin Tsiolkovsky published a book that he claimed scientifically proved that space travel was possible. In 1933, Sergei Korole headed the Soviet team that launched the first Soviet rocket. The flight lasted 18 seconds.

The Soviets did much better on October 4, 1957, when they surged ahead of the United States in the space race by launching *Sputnik I*, the world's first satellite. Over the next four years, the Soviets put the first dog (Laika in 1957), the first man (Yuri Gagarin in 1961), and the first woman (Valentina Tereshkova in 1963) into space. Although the United States was first to put a man on the moon, a feat the Soviets never duplicated, the Soviets had many other firsts in space over the years. Their last major triumph was launching the Mir (Peace) space station in 1986. This invaluable space laboratory, still in use, has hosted astronauts from other countries, including the United States.

Since independence, Russia has been unable to maintain the Soviet space program. In fact, the Baikonur Space Center, the most important Soviet launching site, is in Kazakhstan. Today it is a sad place, starved of the money it needs to keep Russia's program moving forward. Two 170-million horse-power Energia rockets, the most powerful in the world, sit silently in a huge building littered with bird droppings and feathers, sad reminders of the only things that are flying at the center. In a nearby building are two Buran spacecraft. The Buran is the Russian version of the U. S. space shuttle. Built at a cost of $29 billion, the Buran has flown only once. It was an unmanned flight in which Buran landed less than 3 feet (1 meter) from where it was supposed to land.

In 1995 the Russian space program received only $300 million, as opposed to $14 billion for the U. S. program. Yuri Koptev, the director of the Russian Space Agency, summed up what is at stake for Russian science:

> It would be sad, strange, and confusing if the space program were folded in this country. Especially for those of us who have been concerned with these matters for dozens of years, but also for anyone in Russia, it would be demoralizing if our work suddenly ended and our accomplishments were denied.[28]

Koptev might have added that the rest of the scientific world would lose as well. In fact, the situation is not completely grim.

While Russia's space program is suffering at home, Russian space technology is finding a profitable market abroad. The main reason is that during the Cold War the Soviet Union developed liquid-fueled rocket engines unmatched anywhere else, including the United States. As a result, Russia today has several rocket engines that are more powerful, more reliable, and cheaper than those of any foreign competitor. They are ideal for launching commercial satellites such as those used in the booming business of telecommunications. Several American rocket companies will use Russian-made engines in their new projects, including Lockeed Martin Corporation, the world's largest military and aerospace contractor. The Pratt and Whitney company is working with a Russian company to develop a new rocket based on a proven Russian design. So it seems that the high-tech products developed largely for domestic military uses are becoming one of Russia's first and most important international commercial successes.

Tallinn
Capital and largest city in Estonia (population: 484,000). While Estonians were the first to settle the large hill that overlooks Tallinn, the city really dates from the Danish conquest of the region in the thirteenth century. German merchants turned the city into a major trading center, linking the Russian hinterland with Europe to the west. Furs, leather, and seal fat all passed through city, which was best known by its German name, Reval, until the early twentieth century. In 1346 the Danes sold the northern part of Estonia, including Tallinn, to the German Livonian knights. Tallinn continued to prosper until the sixteenth century, when the Baltic region became a battleground between Sweden, Poland, and Russia.

Russian control after 1710 eventually brought growth and, in the nineteenth century, industrialization.

It was during the nineteenth century that Estonians finally became a majority of Tallinn's population. However, that majority did not survive the era of Soviet rule, and as of the mid-1990s about half of Tallinn's population was Russian-speaking.

After suffering extensive destruction in World War II, Tallinn again expanded and industrialized. It was the Soviet Union's main port for handling grain. Beginning in the 1960s, the city's Russian population grew because of large-scale immigration, to the dismay of native Estonians. Despite wartime destruction and Russian and Soviet building, much of medieval old Tallinn, with its winding cobbled streets, picturesque houses, and needlelike spires, still stands. Only 53 miles (85 kilometers) away just across the Gulf of Finland is Helsinki, the capital of Finland.

Tashkent

Capital of Uzbekistan and Central Asia's largest (population: more than 2 million) and most European city. Taskhent means "city of stone." It was the fourth-largest city in the former Soviet Union and served as Moscow's administrative center for all of Central Asia. Tashkent is home to the library of the fifteenth-century poet and scholar Alisher Navoi, which contains about two million volumes, including many beautiful old illuminated manuscripts. It also is the only Central Asian city with a subway system.

Tatars

Descendants of the Turkic people whose state, the Golden Horde, controlled Russia for more than 200 years. Although the Russians used the term "Tatar" to refer both to the Mongols from eastern Asia and the Turkic tribes who fought with them, today's Tatars, who are Muslims, trace their roots to the latter group. They make up about 3.75 percent of the Russian Federation's population, making them the country's largest single minority group.

Russian expansion beginning in the sixteenth century led to the conquest of the Tatar Khanate of Kazan along the Volga River. Ivan the Terrible commemorated his conquest of Kazan in 1552 by building St. Basil's Cathedral in Moscow. The conquest of Astrakhan, a second Tatar state in the region, followed a few years later, although Russia continued to suffer from raids from a third Tatar state in the Crimean Peninsula. That region did not come under Russian rule until Russia conquered it from the Ottoman Empire during the reign of Catherine the Great.

Over the centuries Russia's Tatars became the most assimilated of the empire's Muslim peoples. There was frequent intermarriage between Russians and Tatars, and many old Russian noble families had Tatar roots. Today, however, the Tatars are undergoing a strong national revival. Tatars are trying to regain their cultural identity, and some want to restore the independence they lost 450 years ago. The center of the revival is Tatarstan, one of Russia's twenty-one ethnic republics, which sits astride the Volga River where the Khanate of Kazan once ruled. (The Tatars of the Crimea were deported from the region by Stalin in 1944 and, while some have returned, today are only a small percentage of the peninsula's population.)

After the collapse of the Soviet Union, Tatarstan took several steps toward becoming what its leaders vaguely called a "sovereign state." They carefully left unsaid exactly what their final goal was. By the mid-1990s, the republic had adopted its own constitution, issued license plates, and even announced a national coat of arms. Tatar, along with Russian, was designated as the region's official language. Unlike Chechnya, however, Tatarstan ultimately stopped short of declaring independence.

That restraint was sensible, and may have spared Tatarstan the same tragic fate as Chechnya. Tatarstan is strategically located and vitally important to the Russian Federation. Major roads, railroads, and oil pipelines all cross the republic's territory. In addition, its population is only about 49 percent Tatar (versus 43 percent Russian). While the Tatar national revival is likely to continue, the government in Moscow will be watching carefully to make sure it remains within limits short of independence.

Tbilisi

Capital and largest city (population: 1.3 million) of Georgia. Tbilisi has been the capital of Georgia for the past 1,400 years. Its importance comes from its location: Tbilisi sits astride and commands the major east-west road in the Trans-Caucasus region. Foreign powers have long fought for control of Tbilisi, especially the Persians and the Turks, who battled over the city continuously from the sixteenth to the eighteenth century. In 1795 the Persians virtually destroyed Tbilisi before being driven out for the final time. Their wrath was so furious that with the exception of restored churches and the fortress and wall of the old town, few buildings dating from before 1795 stand in the city. As one visitor familiar with its history noted, Tbilisi has been "razed to the ground [and had its] identity plundered so often that its existence at all is a miracle."[29]

In the nineteenth century, rebuilding took place under Russian control. As a result, Tbilisi has many graceful pastel-painted buildings similar to those built in Moscow and St. Petersburg during the same period. During the last decades of the Soviet era, Tbilisi—with its interesting shops, good restaurants, friendly people who are not intimidated by the authorities, and thriving black market—had a markedly un-Soviet atmosphere. Today the city, surrounded by high mountains, stretches for about 13 miles (21 kilometers) along the banks of the Kura River.

Ter-Petrosian, Levon A. (1945–)

President of Armenia. Before entering politics, Ter-Petrosian was a scholar who studied ancient Armenian manuscripts. He became involved in politics in 1988 when he helped found the Karabakh Committee, an organization that worked to reunite Nagorno-Karabakh with Armenia. As president, Ter-Petrosian has undermined democracy in Armenia by using fraudulent methods to win elections.

Ulmanis, Guntis (1939–)

President of Latvia. Ulmanis's great-uncle was the last president of Latvia before it was annexed by the Soviet Union in 1940. Ulmanis and his family were deported to Siberia in 1941 (his great-uncle was executed), but were allowed to return to Latvia after World War II. An economist by training, Ulmanis quit the Communist Party in 1989. He was elected president of Latvia by parliament in 1993.

Ural Mountains

The traditional border between Europe and Asia. The Urals stretch for about 1,250 miles (2,000 kilometers) from the frigid Kara Sea in the north to Kazakhstan in the south. Their highest point is only about 6,200 feet (1,890 meters), so passengers on a train passing through the Urals are unlikely even to notice them. The Ural region has been a major iron-producing and industrial center since the eighteenth century. In 1723, Peter the Great founded Yekaterinburg on the eastern slope of the Urals, about 27 miles (43 kilometers) west of where Asia begins, as a factory and fort to exploit the area's natural resources. Just under two centuries later, Tsar Nicholas II and his family were murdered in that city.

One of the largest and most symbolic of Stalin's industrial projects was built in the Urals region: the Magnitogorsk steel complex. Today it is the world's largest steel mill and an inefficient industrial dinosaur whose out-of-date furnaces pollute the air of the city of Magnitogorsk and the surrounding region. A third of the city's 450,000 residents suffer from various respiratory diseases.

The industrial base of the Urals region grew further during World War II when the Soviet government moved more than 1,300 factories and their workers from areas threatened by the invading German armies. The Soviet government continued industrial development in the Urals after the war. In 1957 the region was the scene of a nuclear disaster when a nuclear waste dump exploded.

Vilnius

Capital and largest city of Lithuania (population: 593,000). Vilnius was founded by Lithuania's Grand Duke Gediminas in the 1320s on a site where farming and trade date back well over 1,000 years. Although Lithuanians consider Vilnius the birthplace of their culture, the city also has been a center of Polish and Jewish culture. Polish influence grew strong after the Polish-Lithuanian union of 1569 and the founding of the city's university by Jesuit priests in 1579. The university's library earned a reputation as one of the finest in Eastern Europe; today it has the world's most outstanding collection of Lithuanian books and manuscripts. Vilnius became a leading center of Jewish learning in the seventeenth and eighteenth centuries and was known as the "Jerusalem of Lithuania." In the years just before World War II, half the city's population was Jewish. Almost all the Jews of Vilnius were murdered in the Holocaust.

Both Poland and Lithuania claimed Vilnius (Vilna in Polish) when they became independent in 1918. When Poland seized the city by force in 1920, Lithuania refused to recognize Polish possession and relations between the two countries remained strained until World War II. In fact, during that period most of the population of Vilnius was Polish or Jewish; Lithuanians were a small minority in the city. As of the mid-1990s they made up about 55 percent of the city's population. This is in sharp contrast with most of the country, where ethnic Lithuanians are an overwhelming majority.

During the Soviet era, Vilnius grew and became a high-technology manufacturing center. Much of the city's old town, with more than five centuries of varied architecture, still stands and awaits restoration.

Vladivostok

Russia's main Pacific port (population: 690,000). Vladivostok is seven time zones and almost 6,000 miles (9,600 kilometers) east of Moscow, at the very end of the Trans-Siberian railroad. Built on territory seized from China in 1860, its name means "Lord of the East." After serving as the Russian Empire's main Pacific naval base, Vladivostok became home to the Soviet Union's mighty Pacific fleet. It was closed to all foreigners from 1958 to 1991. The sole major exception was a summit meeting between Leonid Brezhnev and U.S. President Gerald Ford in 1975. The Soviet regime kept the city's residents well supplied with consumer goods as a reward for living in Russia's remote eastern corner opposite Japan.

Since the fall of the Soviet Union, the Pacific fleet and the harbor that houses it have been sorely neglected. There are fewer navy-related jobs than before. However, merchant and fishing ships have brought new jobs to Vladivostok. One of the largest new businesses in the city is importing used cars from Japan. Many are brought in by merchant sailors who sell them in the port for a quick profit. Since Vladivostok was opened to foreigners in 1992, many have started businesses there, and the United States opened up a consulate.

Vladivostok has a relatively mild climate. Temperatures in summer reach 68 degrees Fahrenheit (20 degrees Celsius) and in winter rarely fall below 5 degrees Fahrenheit (-15 degrees Celsius). However, the city is covered by heavy fog in the spring and whipped by typhoons in the summer.

Volga River

The longest river in Europe (2,195 miles, 3532 kilometers), to Russians their "Dear Little Mother." The Volga flows through the heart of Russia. It rises northwest of Moscow, flows eastward to the city of Kazan, and then heads south into the Caspian Sea. The region between the northern section of the Volga and the Oka River was the cradle of the Russian state that developed around Moscow. The battles and wars fought along its shores are deeply interwoven with Russia's troubled history. No battle evokes more emotion than the titanic struggle fought at the city once called Stalingrad (today: Volgograd), where the Volga makes its last southeastward turn toward the Caspian Sea. It was here in late 1942 and early 1943 that the Soviet army, fighting with its back to the Volga, defeated the Germans in one of the decisive battles of World War II.

The Volga has been a major transportation artery since pre-Kievian times. In 1952 a canal connected the Volga with the Don River to its west. This completed a water route of rivers and canals that connects Moscow to five seas: the Baltic Sea, the White Sea (in the north, an inlet of the Arctic Sea), the Caspian Sea, the Sea of Azov (adjacent to the Black Sea), and the Black Sea.

Once the Volga River flowed slowly and majestically from its northern sources in Russia's forests to the Caspian Sea in about a week. However, in the 1930s a series of hydroelectric dams turned the river into a collection of stagnant lakes. The Volga's waters now take five years to make the same trip and reach the Caspian Sea choked with industrial pollutants. It will take an enormous effort to restore Russia's "Dear Little Mother" to health.

Voznesensky, Andrei A. (1933–)
One of Russia's leading poets. Voznesensky was active in the struggle for greater artistic freedom in the Soviet Union during the 1960s. Among the people he tried to defend was Aleksandr Solzhenitsyn. Voznesensky's poems are known for their rich and plentiful metaphors. He has long admired the United States and was elected an honorary member of the American Academy of Arts and Letters.

Yakovlev, Vladimir (1945–)
Mayor of St. Petersburg. Yakovlev defeated Anatoly Sobchak's bid for reelection in June 1996. A reformer like his opponent, Yakovlev stressed he would be a hands-on manager and focus more attention on local municipal problems than had Sobchak.

Yavlinsky, Grigory Y. (1952–)
Liberal and reformist politician and Harvard-trained economist. Yavlinsky is one of Russia's post-Soviet generation of leaders. He rose to prominence as the main author of Mikhail Gorbachev's "500-Day" economic reform plan, which the Soviet leader never implemented. After 1991 he became one of the leaders of the reformist Yabloko Party and Russia's most popu-

lar reformist politician. He became critical of Boris Yeltsin's reform program, which he says has "liberated the Soviet system instead of liberating society from the Soviet system."[30] He was criticized by reformers for refusing to support Yeltsin in the 1996 presidential election. Instead, Yavlinsky weakened his political standing when he ran as a candidate in the first round and won only about 7 percent of the vote.

Yeltsin, Boris N. (1931–)

President of Russia. Boris Yeltsin was born on February 1, 1931, in the village of Butka near the city of Yekaterinburg (Soviet era name: Sverdlovsk). As he wrote in his autobiography, his mother's and father's families were people who for generations had "plowed the land, sown wheat, and passed their lives like all other country people."[31] Boris got off to a rocky start, setting a pattern that would

repeat itself during his life. At his baptism the officiating priest, who was drunk, dropped the baby boy into the baptismal tub and forgot to take him out. He lay underwater at the bottom of the tub until his mother noticed what had happened, screamed, and pulled her child out. Once the baby was safely retrieved, the priest calmly, and prophetically, said: "Well, if he can survive such an ordeal, it means he's a good tough lad—and I name him Boris."[32]

Yeltsin indeed proved to be tough. He lived with his family of six—and a goat—in a one-room hut. His father, a construction worker, beat him with a belt. Boris was, he admitted, "something of a hooligan," although he also was a good student.[33] His broken "boxer's nose" is the result of a brawl in which he was hit in the face with a cart axle. Boris also was reckless. As a boy he tried to disassemble a stolen hand grenade with a hammer. The explosion that followed cost him two fingers of his left hand.

Young Boris had his principles and was not afraid to stand up for them. At his graduation, he publicly criticized a teacher for treating students badly. That incident nearly cost him the chance to continue his education. But Boris managed to attend the Urals Polytechnic school, become a civil engineer, and work in construction from 1955 for more than a decade. He joined the Communist Party in 1961 and eventually moved from construction to full-time party work. He rose through the ranks and in 1976 was appointed head of the Sverdlovsk regional party organization.

In 1985, Yeltsin was promoted by Mikhail Gorbachev to head the Moscow party organization, the most important in the country. The next year he was appointed to the Politburo, but in 1987, when he criticized other party leaders, including Gorbachev, for moving too slowly on reform, he was fired from all his posts.

He began his comeback in spectacular fashion in 1989 when he was elected to the newly created Congress of People's Deputies with 89 percent of the vote. In 1990, Yeltsin was elected to another new parliament, the parliament of the Russian republic, which shortly thereafter chose him as Russia's president. A month later, in June 1990, Yeltsin struck back at Gorbachev when he used the Communist Party's 28th Congress to announce his resignation. After making a short speech and declaring he was quitting, he marched directly out of the hall, leaving a stunned Gorbachev and 4,700 delegates behind. In June 1991, Yeltsin again was elected president of Russia, but this time in a nationwide election, thereby becoming his country's first popularly elected leader in its eleven-hundred year history.

The event that brought Yeltsin to Russia's political center stage was the August 1991 coup against Mikhail Gorbachev. Yeltsin was eating breakfast in his country cottage when news of the coup reached him. After meeting with supporters (including, at that time, Ruslan Khasbulatov), Yeltsin prepared to go to Moscow. As he got into his car he received some advice and an evaluation of the situation from his daughter that might have unnerved a lesser man: "Papa, keep calm," she said. "Everything depends on you."[34]

The pattern of Yeltsin's life has not changed since he became president of an independent Russia. It has been filled with ups and downs. He has been bold and courageous, and reckless and foolish. He has had significant victories and embarrassing defeats. In the beginning of 1996 he was extremely unpopular, and it seemed impossible that he could win reelection. Yet he rebounded once again and won a decisive victory in the runoff against Communist candidate Gennadi Zyuganov. However, the strenuous campaigning exhausted Yeltsin, who has heart disease, and it was questionable whether he would be able to complete his second term. Yeltsin underwent a successful heart bypass operation at the end of the year.

Yerevan

Armenia's capital and largest city (population: 1.2 million). Yerevan dates from the eighth century B.C., when it was a town in the pre-Armenian state of Urartu. It is situated on a plain about 3,000 feet (914 meters) above sea level and is surrounded by mountains. In the northwestern part of the city is a massive monument to the victims of the 1915 genocide by the Turks against the Armenian people. It includes a needle pointing skyward, symbolizing revival; an eternal flame; and a wall with relief scenes depicting the massacre.

Yevtushenko, Yevgeny (1933–)

A leading poet of the post-Stalin Soviet era. Yevtushenko was one of the most important literary figures in the struggle to expand artistic freedom in the Soviet Union during the Khrushchev era. He achieved international fame with his poems "Babi Yar" (1961), perhaps the first open denunciation of Soviet anti-Semitism, and "The Heirs of Stalin" (1962), which attacked both Stalin and those who collaborated with him. During the Brezhnev years, Yevtushenko defended arrested dissident writers such as Andrei Siniavsky and Joseph Brodsky. His poem "Half Measures" (1989) warned Mikhail Gorbachev that his reforms were not going far enough. "Half freedom is perilous," Yevtushenko wrote, "and saving the Motherland halfway will fail."[35]

Zhirinovsky, Vladimir (1946–)

"I will raise Russia off its knees," Vladimir Zhirinovsky told the Russian people during the parliamentary elections in 1993.[36] Born in Almaty, Kazakhstan, Zhirinovsky, the most flamboyant and the most successful of Russia's extreme nationalist politicians, opposes democracy and is a vicious anti-Semite. He first made his mark on the Russian political scene when he finished third, with 7.8 percent of the vote, in the 1990 presidential elections. His misnamed Liberal Democratic Party—the party rejects both liberal and democratic ideas—scored a stunning upset by winning 23 percent of the vote in the 1993 parliamentary elections, more than any other party. In parliament he behaved outlandishly, often screaming

insults at other deputies. In the 1995 elections, the LDP again surprised most observers by finishing second in the party with more than 11 percent of the vote. While the LDP did poorly in the single-seat districts in 1995, winning only one seat, Zhirinovsky touted himself as a presidential candidate. However, he did poorly in the June 1996 presidential election, winning only 6 percent of the vote. While many Russians consider Zhirinovsky a clown who will never reach the presidency, the continued strength of the LDP is a measure of the discontent in Russia and the disillusionment that millions feel regarding both democracy and free-market economics.

Zhvanetsky, Mikhail (1934–)

One of Russia's best-known humorists. Zhvanetsky's ironic humor often has been compared to that of Woody Allen. In his early sixties during the Soviet era, he was a penetrating critic of communism. Despite his obvious dismay at the results of the 1995 parliamentary elections, Zhvanetsky laughed when a reporter asked for his comment and said, "I always respect the monstrous choices of my people."[37]

Zyuganov, Gennadi (1944–)

Leader of the Communist Party of the Russian Federation. Zyuganov was born in a tiny agricultural village about 250 miles (400 kilometers) south of Moscow near the city of Orel, a provincial capital. Both of his parents were schoolteachers. From his earliest days Zyuganov was an enthusiastic activist in the Communist system. As a schoolboy he led squads of children to pick potatoes at a nearby collective farm.

Zyuganov joined the Communist Party while serving in the army. After his military service he returned to Orel with plans to be a mathematics and science teacher. However, he left teaching and became a full-time Communist Party official instead, beginning as a leader of the local party youth organization. Zyuganov was promoted to a mid-level post in Moscow in 1983, but by the time he rose much higher in the party in the late 1980s, the organization that had run his country since 1917 was close to collapse.

Zyuganov was among the vast majority of the Communist Party officials who bitterly opposed Mikhail Gorbachev's reforms. In 1990 he left the dying Soviet Communist Party to help form a new group based in Russia—the Communist Party of the Russian Federation. He played a central role in working out an ideology that would appeal to a broad spectrum of people opposed to the policies of Gorbachev, and later Yeltsin. In the summer of 1991 leaders in the new party published a fierce attack on Gorbachev called *A Word to the People*. It accused Gorbachev and his allies of destroying the country. The manifesto warned: "Our home is already burning to the ground...the bones of the people are being ground up, and the backbone of Russia is snapped in two."[38]

While several of the authors of *A Word to the People* were involved in the August 1991 coup against Gorbachev, Zyuganov was not. This left him in a position to work and organize when, after the coup's failure, Boris Yeltsin banned the Communist Party of the Soviet Union (CPSU). By then many CPSU officials already were using their connections and positions to take advantage of Yeltsin's privatization programs to make themselves rich. However, Zyuganov and a smaller group remained true to the cause they had served their entire lives. In 1992, Russia's constitutional court ruled that Zyuganov and his comrades could begin organizing Communist parties on a local and regional level. In February 1993, Zyuganov, who had never risen to the top leadership ranks of the old CPSU, was elected chairman of the Communist Party of the Russian Federation.

Zyuganov once again stood on the sidelines during the October 1993 coup against Yeltsin. By then he was well on his way to forging a new identity and ideology for the party. He drew from two sources: conventional Communist beliefs and traditional Russian nationalism. Russian nationalism and patriotism have roots that run far deeper into his country's past than communism or Marxism. In fact, Zyuganov should not be viewed simply as a Marxist; he belongs to a Russian intellectual tradition dating from the 1830s called *Slavophilism*. According to Slavophile thinking, Russia is a civilization distinct from the West. While Western civilization is based on rationalism and individualism, Russian culture is based on Orthodox spirituality and collectivism. That is why Zyuganov could write in his book *Beyond the Horizon*: "Capitalism does not fit the flesh and blood, the customs or the psychology of our society. Once already it caused a civil war. It is not taking root now, and it will never take root."[39]

Zyuganov's ideology, drawing from both sources, also included strong support for the Russian Orthodox Church, hatred of the West for allegedly causing Russia's problems, a rejection of both capitalism and democracy as unsuited to Russia's traditions, and unmistakable manifestations of anti-Semitism.

In December 1993, Zyuganov emerged as a major player on the Russian political scene when the CPRF made a strong showing in the parliamentary elections. Two years later his party's victory in parliamentary elections established him as the main challenger to Boris Yeltsin in the June 1996 presidential elections. Despite an early lead in the polls, Zyuganov was decisively defeated in the election. Still, he and the CPRF remain a powerful force in Russian political life. When a leading Russian politician with democratic views was asked what the West should do in the face of the strength of Zyuganov and the CPRF, he answered, "Wait and tremble."[40]

SOURCE NOTES

HISTORICAL SECTION

Chapter Two
1. Quoted in Nicholas Riazandovsky, *A History of Russia*, 4th edition (New York and Oxford: Oxford University Press, 1984), p. 3.
2. Quoted in Murry Feshback and Alfred Friendly, Jr., *Ecocide in the USSR* (New York: Basic Books, 1992), p. 15.
3. Quoted in Richard Sakwa, *Russian Politics and Society* (London and New York: Routledge, Chapman, and Hall, 1993), p. 205.

Chapter Three
1. Quoted in Diuk and Karatnycky, *New Nations Rising: The Fall of the Soviets and Challenge of Independence* (New York: John Wiley, 1993), p. 71.
2. Quoted in David R. Maples, *Ukraine Under Perestroika: Ecology, Economics, and Workers' Revolt* (New York: St. Martin's Press, 1991), p. 72.
3. Quoted in Abraham Brumberg, "Not So Free At Last," New York Review of Books, October 22, 1992.
4. *The New York Times*, June 12, 1993.
5. Quoted in Roman Solchanyk, "Ukraine," in *Problems of Post Communism*, November-December 1995, pp. 49–50.

Chapter Four
1. Quoted in Michael Urban and Jan Zaprudnik, "Belarus: A Long

Road to Nationhood," in *Nations and Politics in the Soviet Successor States*, edited by Ian Bremmer and Ray Taras (Cambridge and New York: Cambridge University Press, 1993), p. 102.

2. Edward Crankshaw, *Khrushchev: A Career* (New York: Viking, 1966), p. 141.

3. *The New York Times*, May 21, 1993.

Chapter Five

1. Quoted in Diuk and Karatnycky, p. 120.

2. Quoted in Ulf Pauli, *The Baltic States in Facts, Figures and Maps* (London: Janus Publishing Company, 1994), p. 21.

Chapter Six

1. *The New York Times*, October 19, 1995.

2. Ronald Suny, *Armenia in the 20th Century* (Chico, CA: Scholars Press, 1983), p. 41.

Chapter Seven

1. Quoted in Diuk and Karatnycky, p. 186.

2. *The New York Times*, April 6, 1996.

3. Quoted in Diuk and Karatnycky, p. 186.

4. *The New York Times*, April 16, 1995.

5. Quoted in Annette Bohr, "Turkmen," in Graham Smith, editor, *The Nationalities Question in the Soviet Union* (London and New York: Longman, 1990), p. 236.

6. *The New York Times*, April 16, 1995.

7. *Ibid.*

8. Quoted in Gene Husky, "Kyrgyzstan: The Politics of Frustration," in *Nations and Politics in the Soviet Successor States* (Cambridge and New York: Cambridge University Press, 1993), p. 409.

9. Quoted in Annette Bohr and Simon Crisp, "Kyrgyzstan and the Kyrgyz," in *The Nationalities Question in the Post-Soviet States* (London and New York: Longman, 1990), p. 394.

10. Quoted in Murial Atkin, "Tajikistan: Ancient Heritage, New Politics, in *Nations and Politics in the Soviet Successor States*, p. 376.

SOURCE NOTES

ENCYCLOPEDIA SECTION

1. Quoted in *The New York Times*, November 5, 1993.
2. *The Boston Globe*, February 19, 1995.
3. *The New York Times*, May 9, 1993.
4. *Time*, May 27, 1996, p. 62.
5. *The New York Times*, January 26, 1996.
6. *Ibid*.
7. *The New York Times*, April 16, 1995.
8. *The New York Times*, May 6, 1996.
9. *The New York Times*, October 13, 1995.
10. Bertram Wolfe, *Three Who Made a Revolution* (New York: Delta, 1964), p. 17.
11. *The New York Times*, July 17, 1994.
12. *The New York Times*, December 12, 1995.
13. *The New York Times*, November 23, 1995.
14. *Ibid*.
15. *The New York Times*, March 5, 1995.
16. *The New York Times*, December 12, 1995.
17. *The New York Times*, January 13, 1996.
18. *The New York Times*, March 21, 1996.
19. *The New York Times*, May 2, 1992.
20. *The New York Times*, March 23, 1993.
21. *The New York Times*, January 21, 1994.
22. *The New York Times*, June 3, 1993.

23. *Ibid.*
24. Quoted in Michael Kort, *The Soviet Colossus: History and Aftermath*, 4th edition (Armonk, NY and London: M.E. Sharpe, 1996), p. 327.
25. *The Boston Globe*, September 15, 1993.
26. Quoted in Farley Mowat, *The Siberians* (New York: Dutton, 1961), p. 18.
27. *The New York Times*, October 13, 1993.
28. Peter Nasmyth, *Georgia: A Rebel in the Caucasus* (London: Cassel, 1992), p. 65.
29. *The New York Times*, March 21, 1995.
30. *The New York Times*, December 1, 1995.
31. Boris Yeltsin, *Against the Grain: An Autobiography*, translated by Michael Glenny (New York and London: Summit Books, 1990), p. 21.
32. *Ibid.*
33. David Remnick, *Lenin's Tomb: The Last Days of the Soviet Empire* (New York: Random House, 1993), p. 433.
34. *Ibid.*
35. Yevgeny Yevtushenko, "Half Measures," in *Twentieth Century Russian Poetry, Silver and Steel: An Anthology*, selected, with an introduction by Yevgeny Yevtushenko (New York: Doubleday, 1994), p. 819.
36. *The New York Times*, December 14, 1993.
37. *The New York Times*, December 24, 1994.
38. Quoted in David Remnick, "Hammer, Sickle, and Book," *The New York Review of Books*, May 23, 1996, p. 46.
39. Quoted in Alessandra Sanley, "The Hacks Are Back," *The New York Times Magazine*, May 26, 1996, p. 32.
40. Remnick, p. 51.

INDEX

ABOUT THE AUTHOR

Michael G. Kort is a professor of Social Science at Boston University. He is also an expert on the history of the Soviet Union and is the author of college and young adult textbooks on the subject. Dr. Kort has a wide range of interests, as evidenced by some of his other titles for The Millbrook Press, including *China Under Communism*, a New York Public Library Books for the Teen Age selection, *The Cold War*, and, most recently, *Yitzhak Rabin: Israel's Soldier Statesman*, also a New York Public Library Books for the Teen Age selection.

The author lives with his wife and two daughters in Massachusetts.